studies in structure

*the
stages
of
the
spiritual
life
in
four
modern
authors*

Robert J. Andreach

studies

in

structure

Fordham University Press

1964

For Constance, Kevin, and Jason

Acknowledgments

I wish to thank the following for permission to quote: Burns and Oates Ltd. and The Newman Press for *The Complete Works of St. John of the Cross*, trans. and ed. E. Allison Peers.

Doubleday and Company, Inc. for *The Confessions of St. Augustine*, trans. John K. Ryan, copyright © 1960 by Doubleday and Company, Inc.

Farrar, Straus and Company, Inc. for *The Elder Statesman*, copyright © 1959 by T. S. Eliot.

Harcourt, Brace and World, Inc. for *After Strange Gods*, copyright 1934 by Harcourt, Brace and Company, Inc.; *The Complete Poems and Plays of T. S. Eliot: 1909-1950*, copyright 1930, 1958 by T. S. Eliot, 1934, 1952 by Harcourt, Brace and Company, Inc.; *The Confidential Clerk*, copyright 1954 by T. S. Eliot; *The Idea of a Christian Society*, copyright 1940 by T. S. Eliot; and *Selected Essays of T. S. Eliot*, new ed., copyright 1932, 1950 by Harcourt, Brace and Company, Inc.

Liveright Publishing Corp. for *The Collected Poems of Hart Crane*, ed. Waldo Frank, copyright © R 1961 by Liveright Publishing Corp.

Oxford University Press for *The Journals and Papers of Gerard Manley Hopkins*, ed. Humphry House and Graham Storey, copyright © 1959 by the Society of Jesus; *The Letters of Gerard Manley Hopkins to Robert Bridges*, ed. C. C. Abbott, rev. ed., copyright by the Reverend J. Meskell, S. J., and the Society of Jesus; *Poems of Gerard Manley Hopkins*, *acknowledgments*

3rd ed., enl. and ed. W. H. Gardner, copyright by the Reverend J. Meskell, S. J., and the Society of Jesus; and *The Sermons and Devotional Writings of Gerard Manley Hopkins,* ed. Christopher Devlin, S. J., copyright © 1959 by the Society of Jesus.

The Viking Press and Jonathan Cape Ltd. for *A Portrait of the Artist as a Young Man,* new ed., illus. ed., copyright 1916 by B. W. Huebsch, 1944 by Nora Joyce.

Brom Weber for *The Letters of Hart Crane: 1916-1932,* ed. Brom Weber, copyright 1952 by Brom Weber.

I also wish to thank Professor Oscar Cargill of New York University for his assistance and encouragement throughout the writing of the manuscript and the University of Rhode Island for a research grant-in-aid for the typing of the manuscript.

All references to the following works are included in the text: Crane's letters as (//), Hopkins' poems as (#), and Joyce's *Portrait* as ( ).

In this book I use the Jonathan Cape edition of Joyce's *Portrait,* new ed. 1924, illus. ed. 1956. About the time my manuscript reached the galley stage, The Viking Press published its definitive edition, corrected by C. G. Anderson, ed. Richard Ellmann, 1964. The page differences are as follows:

		Cape	Viking
Chapter	I	7	7
	II	61	60
	III	104	102
	IV	150	147
	V	177	174

Contents

studies in structure

I

Introduction

I DO NOT THINK THAT ANYONE WILL DISPUTE THE STATEMENT
that modern literature is deeply spiritual. What debate there
is centers around the nature of the spiritual experience in an
author's work or, more specifically, his Christian commitment.
This study, then, is an examination of the structure, the
stages of the spiritual life, in certain of the writings of Gerard
Manley Hopkins, James Joyce, T. S. Eliot, and Hart Crane,
four modern authors who are clearly writing in a spiritual
frame of reference. To define the experience in their art
should give us exceptional insight into the Western tradition
and modern literature.

Since the Incarnation with Its extension, the Redemption
and membership in the Mystical Body of Christ, is the central
mystery of Christianity, we can determine an author's commitment by studying his work to see not only if it embodies
the mystery but also if it embodies what man must do in relation to the mystery to be in the way of salvation. What man
must do implies a progression from a beginning toward an
end; before one can commence to imitate Christ, he must

1

know Who Christ is and who he is. Recognizing this, the
Church Fathers and later theologians have established steps
which the Christian can take to grow spiritually so that he
will become more receptive to God's grace, which assists him
in further growth. One problem, though, is that to many
people spiritual growth is synonymous with mysticism, a
handy nebulous word for any spiritual experience we do
not bother to understand. Therefore I will use *stages*, or *degrees*, of the spiritual life, better terminology than *ascetic
way* or *mystic way* because of the controversy surrounding
the precise meaning of each and the precise area to which
each refers. And whereas the *ascetic way* is the best term to
describe Hopkins' mature poetry and the *mystic way* is the
term best suited to describe the scheme of *The Bridge*, this
study is concerned with the ground common to all four
authors.

To prevent confusion, I have adopted the argument of
Fr. de Guibert, which bypasses the disagreement surrounding
ascetical theology and *mystical theology*.[1] After showing how
various authorities interpret these terms, he indicates his
preference for the term *spiritual theology:*

> Since each of these three distinctions between ascetical and
> mystical is used by many authors, it is not possible to find
> any one division which is acceptable by common consent.
> This gives rise to the custom of dealing, in one and the same
> treatise, with all the questions that concern both, no matter
> how the distinction between them is understood. More and
> more every day the term "Spiritual Theology" is coming into
> use, since it has the advantage of including under one head-
> ing both ascetical and mystical, and of not supposing that a
> precise and clear-cut distinction exists between them. This
> term explains that the science of the spiritual life is a part of
> theology, that ascetical and mystical cannot be separated,
> and finally, that both have a common purpose, the spiritual
> perfection of man. So it seems that we should follow this

2

usage here. Thus we can deal with matters which some treat as ascetical, while others treat them as mystical, without our inquiring whether any one subject belongs to ascetical or to mystical theology.[2]

The difficulty in separating absolutely mysticism and asceticism is also attested to by Fr. Goodier.[3] Even Fr. Parente, who examines the two subjects in separate treatises and who insists on the distinction between the two, points out that "an ascetic is always an ascetic; the mystic is a mystic only when actually engaged in some form of mystical experience. At other times he must practice virtue, deny himself, pray like every ascetic."[4] He concludes, "the fact remains that mysticism is not a substitute for asceticism, except in contemplation, where God takes the initiative, and He alone decides about the time, the duration, the place of contemplation. In everything else the ascetical life of the soul continues unchanged."[5]

Although in the *Theology* Fr. de Guibert discusses the three stages as degrees of the spiritual life, I will use the terms *purgative way, illuminative way,* and *unitive way* as well as the terms *the degree of beginners, the degree of proficients,* and *the degree of the perfect* because "the fundamental theological principles, ascetical and mystical, should be and are the same. . . . This unity in the midst of variety needs to be emphasized at the outset; for while allowing for these differences there is danger of imagining a kind of rivalry, or antithesis, or exclusiveness between them, setting one 'school' against another."[6] The use of these six terms, plus Miss Underhill's terminology, should not present a problem because the unitive way, or the degree of the perfect, does not appear in the poetry of Hopkins and Eliot, and Joyce's treatment of the stages in the *Portrait* needs lengthy explanation. A form of the unitive way does appear in *The Bridge,* in the "Atlantis" section, but it is not the *experimental perception of*

God's presence in the soul, in the sense in which the commentators referred to in the first three chapters use this definition. What it is will be discussed in the chapter on Crane. And the purpose of this study is not to decide which author is more ascetical than mystical and which is more mystical than ascetical, although a general distinction between mysticism and asceticism in terms of passivity as opposed to activity must be maintained when investigating the difference between Hopkins' early poetry and his mature poetry and between certain of Eliot's poems, especially "A Song for Simeon" and "The Dry Salvages." The purpose is to discover the ground common to all four artists and to establish what meanings the uses of the stages, or degrees, or ways, elicit. In short, this is a work of literary criticism, not theological inquiry.

It must be stated here unequivocally that not one of these men is a mystical poet as I understand the meaning of that term. Since the experience of the mystic is the unitive way of infused contemplation, or the experimental perception of God's presence in the soul, which sets him off from other men, it is imperative that we recognize that the state of infused contemplation is not presented in their works, and, therefore, they are not mystical poets, a designation which all too frequently means almost anything to anyone: Keats, Shelley, Coleridge, Tennyson, Wordsworth, Browning, Whitman, and Blake are among poets offered as examples. I agree with Richard Coanda, when he writes, "Mystical poetry, then, is that poetry which is so rich, intense, God-centered and beyond the realm of ordinary human experience that its author must have been a mystic in order to write it." [7]

Of the four writers whose works are examined in this study, Hopkins is the only one who presents a momentary difficulty, simply because of the frequency with which some form of the word *mystic* (whether affirming or denying its relevance) is encountered in Hopkins studies.[8] If a mystic is one who experiences infused contemplation—"We apply the word mystic to those supernatural acts or states which our own industry is powerless to produce, *even in a low degree, even momentarily*" [9]—and a mystical poet is one who translates this experience into poetry, then Hopkins is not a mystical poet. Unfortunately, John Pick's conclusion of twenty years ago has not been universally accepted: "Not a single line of Hopkins that is extant bears the authentic stamp of the very essence of the Dark Night of the Senses or of the Soul." He then adds, "I have said that Hopkins was not a mystical writer or a mystical poet. This is not to deny that he may have been a mystic, for he may never have expressed that which constitutes the essence of the mystic: the immediate awareness of God's presence in the soul." [10]

The question arises, where did these four men get the material on which they have constructed their work? If they were medieval artists, there would be no question, but because they are modern, living in a secular world, the question is inevitable. The most obvious answer is their own spiritual growth, but since I have no desire to attempt the impossible task of determining which ones did or did not personally experience the stages, we will look elsewhere. The sources of the spiritual life are Sacred Scripture; the documents of the teaching Church; the writings of the Church Fathers, theologians, mystics, and ascetics; hagiography; and tradition. It is not surprising, therefore, that a priest, a man who spent his entire life reacting to the Irish Catholic world view of his youth, a religious poet who set out to place himself within the central tradition of the Western, Christian, world, and a follower of Emerson and Whitman who conceived of his major work as "a mystical synthesis of 'America'" should be familiar with the spiritual life. Anyone influenced by the Bible, or St. Ignatius Loyola, St. Augustine, St. Paul, St. John of the Cross, or St. Thomas

Aquinas would naturally know of the stages. One aspect of the central tradition of the Western world extends from the Greek religious mysteries; through Oedipus' awakening and purgation; medieval romance, with its awakening, purgation as a prerequisite for attaining the Holy Grail, and test at the Perilous Chapel; Parzival's quest; Dante, whose *Commedia* corresponds to the threefold division of the spiritual life; the *Imitation of Christ;* through *Piers Plowman.*

The terms *mystic* and *ascetic* come from the Greeks, the former associated with the mystery cults and the latter in its verb form meaning *to adorn,* later *to practice.* The term *mystical theology,* with the writings of Pseudo-Dionysius (5th c.), passed into the Latin tongue to be used by medieval theologians. *Ascetic* passed into the Latin tongue and the vernacular languages, but although it had been used by St. Paul, Origen, and St. Basil, was replaced by *mystical theology* largely as a result of the influence of Pseudo-Dionysius and not used in the Middle Ages. Because treatises on ascetical theology started to appear in the seventeenth century, efforts began in the next century, which have continued to the present day, to distinguish between mystical and ascetical theology. One final word, the three *degrees* have been in use since the Church Fathers, but it was not until the thirteenth century that the three *ways* were paralleled with them. According to Pourrat:

> The Fathers of the Church graded the spiritual life quite empirically, if we may venture to say so. They distinguished between the beginning, the progress, and the end of its course. Obviously, the counsels and exhortations suited to beginners would be useless to those who were more advanced and to the perfect. Hence, their instructions are adapted to the needs of their hearers....
>
> Especially during the first third of the thirteenth century did Dionysian commentators favour the notion of applying

the threefold division of mystical contemplation to the normal growth of Christian life. . . .

That is the discovery of St. Bonaventure. No doubt the Seraphic Doctor took his inspiration from Thomas Gallus, but went beyond him. It is the general and normal development of the Christian life that he means to explain and not only the soul's ascent towards mystical contemplation. In the purgative way come conversion and purification from sin; in the illuminative way the soul is enlightened as to God and Christ and itself, and tries to imitate the Lord; in the unitive way it is united to God by charity, and abandons itself to the exercise of holy love. St. Bonaventure points out the practices appropriate to each of these three ways.[11]

The threefold division is not the only one. In her syncretic study Miss Underhill argues that this classification is not adequate to describe the process of spiritual growth within mysticism, that in actuality there is a fivefold division. The differences between the two systems will be commented upon only where necessary and possible. For the moment we might offer a simple distinction. Dom Butler merely notes that there is a "vague yet intense longing"[12] that motivates one to grow spiritually, and Fr. de Guibert offers ways in which a desire for spiritual perfection may be aroused.[13] These men are working within the classical framework of purgative, illuminative, and unitive ways. Miss Underhill, however, sees a separate stage, the awakening, preceding the traditional first one.[14] Her second stage, therefore, corresponds to the first stage of the threefold division. In any event, each author will be discussed according to the approach and analysis that best elucidate his work. For example, the *Portrait* reverses the five stages; *The Bridge* follows the normal order of this division.

What is proposed here is a study comparable to those on the metaphysical poets which examine the meaning of their variations on the stages of the devotional life.[15] In each chapter I will establish the common basis, the stages, and then I will investigate the meanings that the variations from this basis elicit. The inclusion of Hopkins is meant to solve a problem. Anticipating a reluctance on the reader's part to accept the possibility of the stages in modern authors, I want to demonstrate that they can form the structure of an artist's work. Hopkins, a priest whose training involved years of discipline based on the Jesuit founder's *Spiritual Exercises*, seems a logical choice for the first chapter.

I intend to show that Hopkins' early poems represent a false direction in that while the language and imagery can be considered as typical of the language and imagery traditionally associated with mystical writings, his poetry at this time is neither mystical nor genuinely ascetical. About the time of his religious conversion, even before his entrance into the Jesuit training, his poetry begins to take the form of the meditation, or the characteristics of ascetical writing. The movement of the mature poems is from the beginners' degree to the major obstacle that prevents the exercitant from reaching the third degree, the test of self-abnegation and humility. Along with the movement from beginner to proficient, purgative to illuminative, the poetry is always and everywhere concerned with the suffering and trials of spiritual growth and the joys that follow from this growth, whether primarily the salvation in self-sacrifice, the union in the Mystical Body of Christ, or secondarily the reclamation of the beauty of nature, the rediscovery of the divine in the natural.

Hopkins must be studied first because his poetry presents orthodox spiritual growth, and unless we see the stages in the writings of a man for whom they are the very marrow of existence, the very reason for his being a priest, we will not understand and appreciate what Joyce, Eliot, and Crane are doing. Until we see genuine purgation and the necessity of humility and charity in the spiritual life, we will miss much of Joyce's irony in the *Portrait*, Chapter IV; until we see the awakening stage in literature, we will not fully understand the inversion of Chapter V of the novel. We need Hopkins to help us understand and appreciate Joyce's and Eliot's treatments of the spiritual life, and we need all three to help us comprehend and evaluate *The Bridge*, which attempts to construct a spiritual life for twentieth-century man.

Hopkins' poetry will be outlined with the main points treated by the other authors emphasized: the sin of pride, which is a deterrent to spiritual growth in "St. Winefred's Well" and "I wake and feel the fell of dark, not day" and which is the cause of Stephen's spiritual inversion in the *Portrait*; the transcendent Reality as opposed to the immanent Reality in *The Bridge*; the reclamation of nature through self-sacrifice in the first group of the later poems and the reclamation of nature in *Ash Wednesday* and of the industrial society through self-sacrifice in the final sections of *The Bridge*; the immature desire to experience infused contemplation in "Nondum," which partially explains the matter of the later poems and which partially accounts for the frustration in Eliot's "A Song for Simeon" and the decision in "The Dry Salvages" section of the *Four Quartets*; and the difference in the significance of the Incarnation in his and Eliot's poetry.

There is a serious caution. At no point is it asserted or implied that Hopkins is the source for these other writers. There are interesting parallels, since the works of the four embody the spiritual life, but this is not a study in any one of the four as a source for any one of the others. When I show parallels between Hopkins and Eliot or Joyce and Eliot, for example, I mean parallels only, not sources.

What is fundamental in Hopkins' work, the sin of pride, which is a hindrance to spiritual growth, becomes in Joyce's *Portrait* the exclusive concern. The novel reverses the stages of the fivefold division of the spiritual life, and, further, within the individual stages, the *Portrait* inverts Stephen's response to, and application of, the matter which constitutes that stage. It can be demonstrated that Joyce inverts the works, which embody the spiritual stages, of three authors he knew: Dante's *Paradiso*, Cantos XIX-XXVI, in Chapter I and *La Vita Nuova* in Chapter V; St. John of the Cross' *Dark Night of the Soul* in Chapters II and IV; and St. Augustine's *Confessions* throughout, but especially in Chapter V. By reversing and inverting the stages, Joyce is intentionally underscoring the spiritual decline of his protagonist.

The similarity of themes in Hopkins' and Eliot's works has never received any kind of thorough treatment. Georges Cattaui offers an introduction; David Morris is primarily interested in imagery, diction, and technical matters; Philip Martin gives a full study, but he confines his attention to *The Wreck of the Deutschland* and *Ash Wednesday*.[16] Yet what is at the heart of the two poets' writings is the suffering and the trials of the spiritual life. In addition, there are the difference in their acceptance of the mystical and ascetical lives and the difference between spiritual growth (Hopkins) and the necessity of the spiritual life for redeeming the earthly life (Eliot).

Along with allusions to Dante, Calvacanti, Rossetti, and others, the ascent in Part III of *Ash Wednesday* has parallels in Stephen's ascent to his room following the hell-fire sermon and in his movements to and from confession in the *Portrait*. Further, the initially unrelated themes of the trials of purgation, hope in the Incarnation, and redemption of man— themes in Hopkins' poems—are shown to be progressively interrelated and then united in the *Four Quartets* and the plays which follow this poem.

It is clear from Crane's letters that *The Bridge* is meant to be a reaffirmation of man's spiritual potentialities, which Crane thought rejected in *The Waste Land*. Crane saw

10

Eliot's poem as pessimistic and a denial of the spiritual life of man. That the mystic way, treated stage by stage in his major poem, lies outside of Christianity is only another point of contrast between him and Eliot.

Finally, this study was done in the belief that a failure to see the uses of the progression of the spiritual life can lead to a distorted interpretation of the *Portrait* and an incomplete interpretation of *The Bridge*. Unless we know the stages, and especially St. John of the Cross's counsels to those in the purgative way, we are liable to make the error Ryf does in his otherwise excellent study of the *Portrait*: "In Chapter IV we see a devout Stephen making a determined effort at a life of mortification, chastity, and devotion." [17] The student of twentieth-century literature has long known of the recurring themes, motifs, symbols, and images in the writings of these men: mystical and ascetical elements, love, the Blessed Virgin, spiritual death, despair, purgation, and so on. This study hopes to clarify the framework of certain of their writings—the stages, or degrees, or ways, of the spiritual life—and the significance of the differences in treatment of the matter of the spiritual life.

II

Gerard Manley Hopkins

HOPKINS' EARLY POETRY IS USUALLY IGNORED EXCEPT FOR occasional references to Pre-Raphaelitism and Pater, aestheticism and sensationalism, Keats and Shelley.[1] Granting the truth of these influences and the restrictions implied, this chapter will begin by showing that the early poetry forms a necessary link in the chain of the corpus of Hopkins' poetry and that our recognition of the unity of these poems, modelled partly on the stages of the mystic way and partly on the meditative tradition, enables us to understand better the powerful effect of St. Ignatius Loyola and the *Spiritual Exercises* on Hopkins after he began his Jesuit training. After examining the early poems as a sequence meant to reproduce the mystic way, I shall then return and examine a few of the poems, 1865-66, as examples of meditative poetry.

There are two early Hopkins poems that exhibit the change of spiritual orientation that characterizes the stage known as the awakening, which, in the words of Miss Underhill, is the "awakening of the Self to consciousness of Divine Reality."[2] While the very early poems, notably

"A Vision of the Mermaids," reveal a heightened perception, they are conventional poems for a young man serving his apprenticeship as a poet. Even "Il Mystico" is more an exercise in writing poetry—the source is Milton's Cherub Contemplation in "Il Penseroso"—than an indication of a profound spiritual experience.

Abruptly, poems 6 and 7 present a new spiritual direction. The titles alone, "New Readings" and "He hath abolished the old drouth," are evidence of a shifting of the spiritual life. The two poems are built upon the contrasts of the pre-awakening period and the awakening stage. "New Readings" opens with a juxtaposition: "Although the letter said" and "I read the story rather." Fecundity in the third stanza is contrasted with sterility in the second stanza. In poem 7 formerly "all was dry"; now "rivers run" and "the field is sopped with merciful dew." The following lines best convey the significance of this new awareness:

> He hath put a new song in my mouth,
> The words are old, the purport new,
> And taught my lips to quote this word
> That I shall live, I shall not die,
> But I shall when the shocks are stored
> See the salvation of the Lord.

Among the unfinished poems and fragments, "Pilate" may be included as representative of the awakening stage in that Pilate admits to spiritual desiccation and a nagging conscience for allowing the crucifixion. He hopes to find atonement in self-crucifixion, but he is not positive about the meaning of the Passion: "But yet they say Christ comes at the last day. / Then will he keep in this stay?"

One of the difficulties in discussing the awakening stage as separate from the purgative stage or any stage other than that of infused contemplation as separate from the

13

others is that the discussion fosters the false notion that there are absolute lines of demarcation between stages. In actuality the stages other than that of infused contemplation overlap. According to Fr. Garrigou-Lagrange, "It is easy to see the logical and vital sequence of the phases through which the soul must pass. It is not a mechanical juxtaposition of successive states, but the organic development of the interior life which thus becomes more and more an intimate conversation of the soul, no longer only with itself but with God." [3] "Pilate" is as much concerned with purgation (and imitation of Christ) as it is with awakening.

Immediately Hopkins' early poetry moves into another stage, although it would be an error to conclude it is the purgative stage. It contains the characteristics of this stage—detachment, mortification, penance, mental prayer, self-discipline, and purification—but only because the progression dictates that the second stage follow the first. These poems lack the fire generated by a true purging of the self. There is no cry of agony wrenched from the lips of one breaking his will. The extent of this superficiality will become manifest when we investigate his later poetry, which returns to the beginning, but, unlike the early poetry, embodies a genuine ascetic purgation.

Of the two poems dealing with the renunciation of profane love for sacred love, "The Beginning of the End" and "A Voice from the World," the second is the more sincere one, for although it is clear that divine love transcends earthly love, the speaker finds the way torturous: "Lord, forgive. / I cannot calm, I cannot heed." In lines not far removed in meaning from passages in Eliot's *Ash Wednesday*, the speaker accepts the purgative way through the assistance of the female:

> Teach me the paces that you went
> I can send up an Esau's cry;

Tune it to words of good intent.
This ice, this lead, this steel, this stone,
This heart is warm to you alone;
Make it to God. I am not spent
So far but I have yet within
The penetrative element
That shall unglue the crust of sin.
Steel may be melted and rock rent.
Penance shall clothe me to the bone.
Teach me the way: I will repent.

He knows that ultimately he must give up "remember'd sweetness" for

Him who gives thee all,
Freely forgives the monstrous debt!
Having the infinitely great
Therewith to hanker for the small!

Poem 10, "The Alchemist in the City," reinforces the quest for detachment (introduced in "Rest" [4]), in the first stanza, in the sharp contrast of the solitary speaker and the dynamic, fluid universe. The fifth stanza hints at what will torment the speaker throughout his entire spiritual journey: his overwhelming sense of man's weakness, his sense of sin. The remainder of the poem deals with the attempt to find solitude among "ancient mounds that cover bones. . . ."

In the next poem the speaker seeks to detach himself, not from society, but from what is more important to him, the sense of selfhood, which stands between him and God: "Myself unholy, from myself unholy." Accepting his sins, which weigh him down—"And so, though each have one while I have all"—he concludes with his soul turned toward "no other / Save Christ: to Christ I look, on Christ I call."

There are four poems which constitute a unit within the larger movement of this simulated mystic way. The first, poem 14, opens with a discordant note. Spring, the season of rebirth and growth, of color and warmth and beauty, "opens with disabling cold, / And hunting winds and the long-lying snow." The questions, "Is it a wonder if the buds are slow? / Or where is strength to make the leaf unfold?" direct the speaker to the sterility of his spiritual life paralleled in nature: "Chilling remembrance of my days of old / Afflicts no less." The seed "which the good sower once did sow" and "which should ere now have led my feet to the field" has not yet been brought to fruition because of "the waste done in unreticent youth."

One of the answers to the question posed in the closing lines of "A Voice" must be prayer, for it is central to spiritual training, to asceticism, to mysticism. In poem 15 the speaker's "prayers must meet a brazen heaven / And fail or scatter all away"; he is "unclean and seeming unforgiven"; he cannot overcome the desires of the self. He "reckons" the meaning and value of God's love, which strengthens and girds the seeker after His love, and he knows that the love which pours out from Him has precedence over earthly love. He "feels," however, the deeply-ingrained nature of sin and his weakness for allowing it "long success." The desires of the self, oriented toward the material world, are not easily subdued. Poem 15 is the first of the completed poems to indicate the struggle for purification: "A warfare of my lips in truth, / Battling with God, is now my prayer."

Poem 16, "Let me be to Thee as the circling bird," is sharply distinguished from the preceding one. It presents a state of joy, the result of finding "the dominant of my range and state— / Love, O my God, to call Thee Love and Love."

"The Half-way House," poem 17, is an advance upon poem 16 in that the opening line refers to a momentary revelation, "Love I was shown upon the mountain-side," and the following lines to a realization of the disparity between the two worlds of becoming and being, temporal and eternal. It is the speaker who must "creep" while Love "on wings dost ride." It "grows darker here" in the world of becoming while "thou art above" in the world of being. There is a note of defeat in the speaker's pleading, "Love, come down to me if thy name be Love." The third stanza presents what is typical of mysticism, paradox, for paradoxicality, according to W. T. Stace, is one of the "universal common characteristics of mysticism in all cultures, ages, religions, and civilizations of the world." [5] In order for the union to occur, "when all is given," the speaker "must see" Love, but "to see" Love in the temporal, spatial world means a bridging of the gap that separates the worlds of God and man because for him Love, the transcendent Reality, exists in the non-temporal, non-spatial world. "To love, love" has a double meaning: 1) in order to love, the speaker needs God's love, and 2) in order to progress spiritually, he must love both God and His creatures. If the speaker "shall overtake" Love "at last above," he "must o'ertake" Love "at once and under heaven" because in the unitive state, or state of infused contemplation, there is the experimental perception of God's presence in the soul, a foretaste of the beatific vision. The poem concludes, not with the unitive way, but with a statement of where such an experience of the Real Presence can occur.

Among the fragments and unfinished poems, poem 96 stands chronologically near poems 22 and 24. It is a transitional poem that moves beyond the "Past, O Past, no more be seen!" There is hope that "the Bethlehem star may lead me / To the sight of Him who freed me / From the self that I have been."

"Nondum" is intermediate between the depression of poem 15 and the joy of "God's Grandeur." It recalls "My prayers must meet a brazen heaven" in that the prayers of "the trembling sinner" receive no divine response: "Our prayer seems lost in desert ways, / Our hymn in the vast silence dies." He can "see the glories of the earth" but "not the hand that wrought them all." Unable to achieve union, he can only "guess; we clothe Thee, unseen King, / With attributes we deem are meet." He has not yet learned that God is to be found within, that the soul can be flooded with grace. Gradually the soul is engulfed in darkness,

> And still th'abysses infinite
> Surround the peak from which we gaze.
> Deep calls to deep and blackest night
> Giddies the soul with blinding daze
> That dares to cast its searching sight
> On being's dread and vacant maze,

which leads me to believe the intention here is to represent the prayer of recollection, which precedes the prayer of quiet, but this is debatable. In stanza seven the speaker silences his lips and quells his "breast's desponding sob." Gazing inward, he can move in a world of silence. His strength is renewed. Having temporarily subdued his sense perceptions and bodily images, he can wait patiently for "that sense beyond," the felt presence of God in his soul:

> Oh! till Thou givest that sense beyond,
> To show Thee that Thou art, and near,
> Let patience with her chastening wand
> Dispel the doubt and dry the tear;
> And lead me child-like by the hand;
> If still in darkness not in fear.

He can find hope in the meaning of Easter—poems 13 and 23 praise the resurrected Christ—for Easter teaches him that salvation follows pain.

"The Habit of Perfection" resolves the tensions of the earlier poems. The speaker rejoices in

Elected Silence, sing to me
And beat upon my whorlèd ear,
Pipe me to pastures still and be
The music that I care to hear.

One by one he purges the five senses, fully aware that only through purification can he grow spiritually. It is only by gazing inward, by stripping away distracting sense perceptions and bodily images, can the "eyes . . . find the uncreated light," can the soul "unhouse and house the Lord," that is, find Him in the tabernacle and make the soul ready for Him. We should note the use of "the uncreated light":

> That Divine Dark, that Abyss of the Godhead, of which he [the mystic] sometimes speaks as the goal of his quest, is just this Absolute, the Uncreated Light in which the Universe is bathed, and which—transcending, as it does, all human powers of expression—he can only describe to us as *dark*.[6]

The speaker elects the religious vow of poverty so that the marriage feast, traditional mystical language for union—a tradition, which, according to Dom Butler, originates with Origen and becomes popular from the time of St. Bernard onwards [7]—can begin:

> And, Poverty, be thou the bride
> And now the marriage feast begun,
> And lily-coloured clothes provide
> Your spouse not laboured-at nor spun.

So far the poems have been read as examples of the spiritual progression known as the mystic way; they trace a progression from awakening to a cessation of the faculties that precedes the mystical experience. Many, however, can be read as examples of meditative poetry.[8] Starting with

19

February-March, 1865, a change occurs in the entries in the early diaries. Among books to be read, Hopkins lists *The Spiritual Combat,* the book of meditative-devotional reading.[9] For March 12, he writes, "A day of the great mercy of God," and then, "I confessed on Saturday, Lady Day, March 25." [10] On page 60 in *The Journals* we read, among other entries, references to *The Divine Master,* a book of devotions based on the Way of the Cross; to Aitken's *Teaching of the Types* (number one is the distinctive character of the natural, the spiritual, and the divine life); to Dr. Pusey on Daniel and his sermon on everlasting punishment and the remedy for sins of the body.

Even though Hopkins did not study the *Spiritual Exercises* until later, we can take—using the approach of Martz and Downes [11]—the *Exercises* as a model of the meditative method. The meditation, or spiritual exercise, is divided into three elements: composition of place, analysis, and colloquy. An examination of three poems will suffice.

In poem 14 the opening lines constitute the composition of place. In the spiritual exercise the second element is a searching into the mystery for its meaning and its application to the individual. It is divided into points. For the first week, first exercise, St. Ignatius explains that "the first point will be to apply the memory to the first sin, which was that of the angels; and then the understanding to the same by reasoning on it; and then the will, desiring to remember and understand the whole...." He continues, "The second point will be to do the same, i.e. to apply the three powers to the sin of Adam and Eve..." and "the third point will be to do in like manner in regard to the third sin, i.e. the particular sin of some one person, who for one mortal sin has gone to hell...." In this poem the section including "Chilling remembrance of my days of old / Afflicts no less, what yet I hope may blow" constitutes the analysis, the application to the individual, and the last line, "Therefore how bitter, and learnt how late, the truth!" while not quite a colloquy, nonetheless brings the truth of the meditation to the speaker.

In poem 17, "The Half-way House," the first stanza is the composition of place; the second can be considered part of the analysis; the third, "Hear yet my paradox," while remaining part of the analysis also begins the colloquy. The poem concludes with the voice directing the suppliant to the Eucharist: "You have your wish; enter these walls, one said: / He is with you in the breaking of the bread."

Finally, poem 22, "Nondum," opens with a preparatory prayer, the usual preliminary to a meditation. The second stanza begins the composition of place: "We see the glories of the earth / But not the hand that wrought them all." Both memory and understanding are initially present in the large middle section which extends to the eighth stanza. Then the will, profiting from the analysis, abandons itself to the divine will, in the stanza beginning, "Oh! till Thou givest that sense beyond." In the final stanza the suppliant asks God to answer his prayer so that he will be allowed to rise above the meditation and receive the mystical experience.

From poem 6 on the awakening stage of Miss Underhill's classification system and a progression leading up to the awaited mystical experience are present in Hopkins' early poetry. Why this is so is perhaps answered by John Wain, after his reading of "The Alchemist in the City": "The fact of his being a Jesuit did not 'cut him off.' He was already cut off by unalterable features of his own temperament." [12] His early poetry can be read in terms of pseudo-mystical progression. (I use the term *pseudo-mystical* to indicate poetry that is neither ascetical nor mystical, yet which tries to duplicate the mystic way by reproducing the stages from awakening through the dark night. On the one hand, it is not genuine ascetical poetry as his mature poetry is; on the other hand, it is not mystical poetry according to the definition in the introduction. Nor is it structure as a technique revealing a larger meaning as in Joyce's *Portrait*.) We do find language and imagery traditionally associated with mysticism: the "paradox," the "blackest night / Giddies the soul with blinding daze," the desire "to behold Thee as Thou art," the "uncreated light," the "marriage feast," and the frequent use of "Love." Even Miss Underhill sees the opening two lines of "God's Grandeur" as the "characteristic expression" [13] of her illumination of the self stage. Today, though, perceptive critics agree that *mysticism* and *mystical poetry* are not accurate terms for Hopkins' poems, for he is pre-eminently a poet of *ascetical theology*, of "prayer, patience, alms, vows" (# 32). Whether it be the purgative way, the degree of beginners, or the illuminative way, the degree of proficients, the later poetry is grounded in the trials, temptations, and obstacles to spiritual growth.

This change from pseudo-mystical to ascetical can be seen in the last of the early poems, "Rosa Mystica," where the speaker turns to one of the great symbols of Catholic mysticism, the rose: "Mary, the Virgin, well the heart knows, / She is the Mystery, she is that Rose." Through her he hopes to find the divine Reality, for the rose is also the symbol of Christ:

> Who can her Rose be? It could be but One:
> Christ Jesus, our Lord—her God and her Son.
> In the Gardens of God, in the daylight divine
> Shew me thy Son, Mother, Mother of mine.

But whereas in the last stanza of "Nondum" the speaker asks God directly for His presence, in "Rosa Mystica" he asks Mary for her assistance. Further, in the earlier poems he seeks God's "hand"; here he asks Mary's aid because in her role as mediatrix of all graces, she is an embodiment of mercy and charity. Through her the speaker may receive, not God directly in the mystical experience, but God's grace:

Does it smell sweet, too, in that holy place?
Sweet unto God, and the sweetness is grace;
The breath of it bathes the great heaven above
In grace that is charity, grace that is love.
To thy breast, to thy rest, to thy glory divine
Draw me by charity, Mother of mine.

It is clear that toward the end of his early period the meditative method begins to shape his poems. True, these early poems are not so precisely meditative as some of the later ones, nor are they great poems. Nor do they present genuine mystical or ascetical purgation. It is his mature poetry that makes him "the acknowledged poet par excellence of the Ignatian Spiritual Exercises." [14] Eventually, though, the more obviously mystical elements are subsumed under a discipline that, we suspect, was much closer to his temperament. We know the direction he took in 1866. In the diary we read, for November 6, 1865, "On this day by God's grace I resolved to give up all beauty until I had His leave for it," and near the end of the diary: "For Lent. No pudding on Sundays. No tea except if to keep me awake and then without sugar. Meat only once a day. No verses in Passion Week or on Fridays. No lunch or meat on Fridays. Not to sit in armchair except can work in no other way. Ash Wednesday and Good Friday bread and water." [15]

We find, then, in Hopkins' poetry a shift from pseudo-mysticism to asceticism, just as we will find a comparable shift, to be qualified later, in Eliot's poetry. This is why, when we examine Hopkins' later poetry, we will encounter the purgative stage again, but a more genuine and ascetic purgation.

Nowhere in the later poems do we find a cluster of mystical elements such as we find in the early poems. The later poetry never progresses beyond the illuminative way, the degree of proficients; it never embodies the prayer of recollection or the prayer of quiet. I do not wish to push too far the following possibility, but the lines, "To see thee I must see thee," in "The Half-way House," and "Oh! till Thou givest that sense beyond, / To show Thee that Thou art, and near" and "Then, to behold Thee as Thou art, / I'll wait till morn eternal breaks," in "Nondum," may be read as a desire to experience infused contemplation. Putting aside the question of who can achieve this state, the student of mysticism and spiritual theology knows that the exercitant normally must first meet the demands of the two earlier states and conquer the obstacles to spiritual growth. In the early poems there is a strong element of youthful, immature mysticism (pseudo-mysticism). There is a desire to race to the last stage and an impatience that the mystical experience has not taken place.

Without a doubt Hopkins' Jesuit training taught him the necessity of spiritual training in the deepest sense, and the distance separating the youthful seeker for God and the older, more humble, ascetic priest can be gauged by contrasting the early line, "To see thee I must see thee," and the magnificent line in one of his last poems, "Mine, O thou lord of life, send my roots rain."

One of the two major influences on Hopkins' mature thought and art is St. Ignatius' *Spiritual Exercises*. It is the sense of sin, triple and personal, and of man's unworthiness that is the desired result of the first four exercises within the first week; it is the sense of the horror of hell with its removal from God that is the subject of the meditation of the fifth exercise of this week. The second point of the first exercise is "to apply the three powers to the sin of Adam and Eve, bringing before the memory how for that sin they did such long penance, and how great corruption came upon the human race, so many men going towards hell." In the third exercise the exercitant is expected to mark and dwell "on the points in which I have felt greater consolation, or desolation, or greater spiritual relish ... ," spiritual states often referred to in discussions of Hopkins' "terrible" sonnets. The first colloquy of the third exercise introduces the Blessed Virgin, the subject of one of his great poems. But it is the colloquy to the first exercise in the first week, while imagining Christ crucified to experience the sense of His love and one's unworthiness, that gives rise to the central theme in Hopkins' spiritual writings and poetry: the "great sacrifice." [16] As we go through the mature poems, we will see that the solution to man's spiritual predicament is his imitation of Christ's "great sacrifice."

Since the imitation of Christ—a characteristic of the second stage, that of proficients, or the illuminative way— is present from *The Wreck* through the remaining poems, it would seem at first glance that the approach of the stages will not hold for Hopkins' poetry. After all, if the early poems do not exhibit the characteristics of a genuine degree of beginners, does his poetry omit this stage? There are two facts that must be borne in mind. The first is the caution mentioned earlier about viewing the stages as being separated one from the others by absolute terminal lines. The second is that in addition to the simultaneous presence of certain matter of the first two stages, there is a definite progression from beginner to proficient to the supreme test of self-abnegation and humility, in the three groups of the later poems as delineated by Gardner in his two-volume study.

Another consideration should be noted. No matter how formal the early poetry is, at least Hopkins had the benefit of practicing within the tradition of the spiritual life. Here, then, is one influence of the Jesuit founder. While studying the *Spiritual Exercises*, the meditations of which correspond to the threefold division of the ascetic way, Hopkins must have grasped the relationship between the progression of the exercises and the progression he was attempting to simulate from poem 6 through "Nondum." There is a tremendous spiritual gulf separating the early poetry and the later poetry, but the structures are the same. The later poetry is the early poetry rewritten, but instead of its being a sequence modelled on an established pattern, it is poetry informed by the spirit of a man living the stages himself. The great insight of Hopkins during his Jesuit training is the importance of man's election of the imitation of Christ. The speaker of "Nondum" cannot initiate the mystical experience, since that is God's decision, but he certainly can prepare his soul for Him.

The Wreck of the Deutschland is a second awakening not only because it intensifies the mild awakening of poems 6 and 7 but because the experience of the nun recalls a similar experience to the speaker: "dost thou touch me afresh? / Over again I feel thy finger and find thee." The clarity of awakening brings the pain of purgation—"The swoon of a heart that the sweep and the hurl of thee trod / Hard down with a horror of height: / And the midriff astrain with leaning of, laced with fire of stress"—but the goal is redemption and rebirth in "the heart of the Host."

Despite the very personal tone of the poems, particularly in the opening stanzas of *The Wreck* and in the last group, Hopkins is concerned with the spiritual life of mankind. His poems go beyond the limits of one man's spiritual struggle, however terrible. The second part of *The Wreck* is an exemplum of the first part. Through self-sacrifice the nun shows the way all men must seek salvation, for all men are brothers: "From life's dawn it is drawn down, / Abel is Cain's brother and breasts they have sucked the same." The last stanza of *The Wreck* is a plea to the nun, now united with Christ, to intercede for the rest of mankind, the souls of men in "unchrist" (# 41).

St. Ignatius explains that because of sin "corruption came upon the human race"; in the language of fragment 119, "corruption was the world's first woe." Once it was different, in the "earth's sweet being in the beginning / In Eden garden" (# 33), but sin has alienated man from God. Sin has also isolated man from nature. Incapable of seeing its beauty, he wantonly destroys it. His "strokes of havoc unselve / The sweet especial scene" (# 43). The extent of fallen man's solipsism is hinted at in the opening lines of "Binsey Poplars," where a favorite image for Christ cannot be perceived by him; he fails to "stress" the mystery of the "leaping sun."

In spite of this, "nature is never spent" (# 31) because God is unchangeable, the creator of nature and beauty and change: "He fathers-forth whose beauty is past change" (# 37). Just as man cannot repair nature by himself (# 43), so he needs God's assistance in order to grow spiritually. He must acknowledge his unworthiness, the fact that he has "lost that cheer and charm of earth's past prime." He must admit that his "make and making break, are breaking, down / To man's last dust, drain fast towards man's first slime" (# 35). At the same time he needs God to "complete thy creature dear O where it fails" (# 40).

God is both masterful and merciful, one of the great themes of *The Wreck*, and the way to Him is through the stages of the spiritual life, through the way of prayer and penance, pain and suffering, through the way of sacrifice and imitation of Christ, "Thou martyr-master" (# 28). Once man knows that the way to salvation lies in spiritual growth, not only can he take hope in spiritual rebirth,

> Man's spirit will be flesh-bound when found at best,
> But uncumbered: meadow-down is not distressed
> For a rainbow footing it nor he for his bones risen
> (# 39),

but embarked on the way of beginners, he becomes conscious of God's nearness and love. Man's searching reaches fruition, and he rushes to meet Him:

These things, these things were here and but the beholder
  Wanting; which two when they once meet,
The heart rears wings bold and bolder
  And hurls for him, O half hurls earth for him off under
    his feet (# 38).

The spiritual world crashes through the natural world—the
sestet to "The Windhover"—but only if man purges and
cleanses himself, especially through prayer, for prayer "for
souls sunk in seeming / Fresh, till doomfire burn all, / . . .
shall fetch pity eternal" (# 41), and only if he imitates
Christ: the theme of *The Wreck*, "The Windhover," and the
other major poems.

The way is made easier for him. The Holy Ghost "over
the bent / World broods with warm breast and with ah!
bright wings" (# 31). Man is "roped with, always," God's
grace (# 28). It is Christ Who has shown him the way. His
"stress" is always present: "it rides time like riding a river";
it is His "stress" that "guilt is hushed by, hearts are flushed
by and melt." His "stress" is "not out of his bliss" but out
of His pain and suffering (# 28). Man's salvation, through
pain and suffering, made possible through the Incarnation
and Redemption, can be found in Him: "To hero of Calvary,
Christ,'s feet— / Never ask if meaning it, wanting it, warned
of it—men go" (# 28). Christ's "great sacrifice" redeems
the man who will also elect the way of self-sacrifice: "Let
him easter in us" (# 28).[17]

The experience of the nun in *The Wreck* is meant to be
a paradigm. She "sees one thing, one; / Has one fetch in her:
she rears herself to divine / Ears." She willingly accepts pain
and suffering,

  Was calling "O Christ, Christ, come quickly":
The cross to her she calls Christ to her, christens
    her wild-worst
  Best,

and sacrifice for "the Master, / *Ipse*, the only one, Christ, King, Head." Her reward is union with Christ and salvation: "Well, she has thee for the pain, for the / Patience." Progressing in his spiritual life, man can now reclaim the beauty of nature, the divine in the natural, a theme that occurs again and again in the poems of the priest justly acclaimed as one of our finest nature poets. In "Spring" the "thrush's eggs look little low heavens"; the "leaves and blooms, they brush / The descending blue; that blue is all in a rush / With richness"; and the "racing lambs too have fair their fling." Even wet and wildness have beauty (# 56). The natural world, however, is never raised above the spiritual world. It never becomes an end in itself, nor does Hopkins' poetry ever slide into pantheism as Crane's poetry does, for God is the creator of nature, the author of beauty (# 59). He is "throned behind / Death with a sovereignty that heeds but hides, bodes but abides" (# 28). Hopkins' most mature expression is poem 61, a poetic translation of the opening two sentences of the Principle and Foundation of the *Spiritual Exercises*. "Mortal beauty" does this:

> keeps warm
> Men's wits to the things that are; what good means—
> where a glance
> Master more may than gaze, gaze out of countenance.

We should appreciate mortal beauty; we should "love what are love's worthiest, were all known; / World's loveliest— men's selves." In answer to the questions, "What do then? how meet beauty?" we should

> Merely meet it; own,
> Home at heart, heaven's sweet gift; then leave, let that alone.
> Yea, wish that though, wish all, God's better beauty, grace.

In a letter dated February 3, 1883, Hopkins wrote to Bridges about the "insight St. Paul gives us" of Christ's life and character: the "great sacrifice." The letter continues:

> This mind he says, was in Christ Jesus—he means as man: being in the form of God—that is, finding, as in the first instant of his incarnation he did, his human nature informed by the godhead—he thought it nevertheless no snatching-matter for him to be equal with God, but annihilated himself, taking the form of servant; that is, he could not but see what he was, God, but he would see it as if he did not see it, and be it as if he were not and instead of snatching at once at what all the time was his, or was himself, he emptied or exhausted himself so far as that was possible, of godhead and behaved only as God's slave, as his creature, as man, which also he was, and then being in the guise of man humbled himself to death, the death of the cross. It is this holding of himself back, and not snatching at the truest and highest good, the good that was his right, nay his possession from a past eternity in his other nature, his own being and self, which seems to me the root of all his holiness and the imitation of this the root of all moral good in other men.[18]

Hopkins emphasizes man's moral nature in the second group of poems. Unlike nature, "That canst but only be, but dost that long— / Thou canst but be, but that thou well dost" (# 58), man has free will: "You there are master, do your own desire" (# 50). Even though his spiritual life can be stunted,

> Ah, the heir
> To his own selfbent so bound, so tied to his turn,
> To thriftless reave both our rich round world bare
> And none reck of world after, this bids wear
> Earth brows of such care, care and dear concern (# 58),

his first obligation is to mend his "fading fire / . . . and vital candle in close heart's vault" (# 50) and to give all to God, as in "Morning Midday and Evening Sacrifice."

Unlike Caradoc, and Joyce's Stephen, who declaims,

> And I do not repent;
> I do not and I will not repent, not repent.
> . . . .
> Henceforth
> In a wide world of defiance Caradoc lives alone,
> Loyal to his own soul, laying his own law down, no law nor
> Lord now curb him for ever (# 105),

and like Margaret Clitheroe, whose "will was bent at God," man should submit his will to God's will, accept God's will, and abandon his will to God's will. He must—"on that path" the boy who strives to "doff darkness" races—"run all your race, O brace sterner that strain!" (# 51) for the universe is reducible to moral right and wrong (# 62).

By serving God analogously as the priest does in "The Bugler's First Communion," he comes to love humanity, to see all men as fellow creatures, each one engaged in the self-sacrifice necessary to return to God: "Felix Randal," "Brothers," "Tom's Garland," "Harry Ploughman," and "Cheery Beggar." Refusal to practice humility, the sin of pride, can lead in only one direction, eternal damnation, "where, selfwrung, selfstrung, sheathe-and shelterless, thoughts against thoughts in groans grind" (# 62).

Since God is both masterful and merciful, man can hope for grace while striving toward spiritual perfection:

> For grace is any action, activity, on God's part by which, in creating or after creating, he carries the creature to or towards the end of its being, which is its selfsacrifice to God and its salvation. It is, I say, any such activity on God's part; so that so far as this action or activity is God's it is divine

stress, holy spirit, and, as all is done through Christ, Christ's spirit; so far as it is action, correspondence, on the creature's it is *actio salutaris;* so far as it is looked at *in esse quieto* it is Christ in his member on the one side, his member in Christ on the other. It is as if a man said: That is Christ playing at me and me playing at Christ, only that is no play but truth; That is Christ *being me* and me being Christ.[19]

"That is Christ *being me* and me being Christ" receives one of its finest detailed poetic expressions in the sonnet "As kingfishers catch fire, dragonflies draw flame." The nearness of grace receives its fullest poetic expression in "The Blessed Virgin compared to the Air we Breathe." Just as we are surrounded by air which sustains our bodies, so "we are wound / With mercy round and round." It is Mary who "plays in grace her part / About man's beating heart." The poem concludes with a plea to her to intercede for man, to stir in his ears, to "speak there / Of God's love, O live air, / Of patience, penance, prayer."

In the third group of poems, poems of desolation and recovery, we get "the war within" (# 73), the contention between man and God. The extent of that struggle is best described in "Carrion Comfort," in the lines:

> But ah, but O thou terrible, why wouldst thou rude on me
> Thy wring-world right foot rock? lay a lionlimb against me? scan
> With darksome devouring eyes my bruisèd bones? and fan
> O in turns of tempest, me heaped there; me frantic to avoid thee and flee?

The cause of that struggle is the persistence of selfhood, the refusal to abandon totally the will to God's will, the failure to achieve complete self-abnegation and humility:

God's most deep decree
Bitter would have me taste: my taste was me;
Bones built in me, flesh filled, blood brimmed the curse.
Selfyeast of spirit a dull dough sours (# 69).

Hence the tremendous onslaught by God in "Carrion Comfort" and the denial of light in "I wake and feel the fell of dark." Spiritual progress can come only if "the rebellious wills / Of us we do bid God bend to him even so" (# 70).

Despite the temporary suspension of hope in "No worst, there is none," God gives man strength in "Carrion Comfort," patience in "Patience, hard thing!" hope and light in "My own heart let me more have pity on." He must combat despair (# 64), for he has not yet been plunged into the hell of poem 69. The world is temporary; nature and man will give way to the spiritual world (# 72). Salvation, made possible through Christ's "great sacrifice," can be his through the desire for spiritual perfection, through the way of prayer, mortification, and purgation, and through the way of imitation of Christ in self-sacrifice. Christ's action will triumph in the man who elects to grow spiritually:

In a flash, at a trumpet crash,
I am all at once what Christ is, since he was what
I am, and
This Jack, joke, poor potsherd, patch, matchwood,
immortal diamond,
Is immortal diamond (# 72).

We are ready to examine the overall structure of Hopkins' mature poetry. According to the commentators on the spiritual life, the goal of the first stage of the threefold division is knowledge of the limited self and knowledge of the loving God, and the means for achieving this goal are mental prayer, mortification, penance, examen of conscience, confession, and the like.[20] There are three themes present in the first group of the later poems. The first one emphasizes the speaker's awareness of man's alienation, through sin, from God. He is caught between "the frown of his face / Before me, the hurtle of hell / Behind" (# 28). In "God's Grandeur" the speaker asks, "Why do men then now not reck his rod?" In "The Starlight Night" this "piece-bright paling shuts the spouse / Christ home," removed from fallen man. Spring, in the poem of that title, is only "a strain of the earth's sweet being in the beginning / In Eden garden." The sea and the skylark "shame this shallow and frail town! / How ring right out our sordid turbid time, / Being pure!" In poem 39 "man's mounting spirit in his bone-house, mean house, dwells." In poem 40 "only the inmate does not correspond." The speaker in "The Loss of the Eurydice" deplores "my people and born own nation, / Fast foundering own generation." "O if we but knew what we do," groans the speaker in "Binsey Poplars." These poems are built upon man's recognition of his fallen nature; that is, they deal with his gaining self-knowledge.

A second theme emphasizes the means of purgation. *The Wreck* directs men "to hero of Calvary, Christ,'s feet." To the question, "Buy then! bid then!—What?" poem 32 replies, "Prayer, patience, alms, vows." The active life of asceticism is implied in "The Windhover," in the passage, "sheer plod makes plough down sillion / Shine." There is the simple injunction, "Praise him," in "Pied Beauty" and the moving prayer in "Valley of the Elwy." Poem 41 offers a more powerful prayer; the suppliant should "crouch; lay knee by earth low under." That man must work toward finding God is clear from "Hurrahing in Harvest," in the lines, "I walk, I lift up, I lift up heart, eyes, / Down all that glory in the heavens to glean our Saviour." The other side to this theme is God's action in helping him, in *The Wreck*, "The Windhover," "God's Grandeur," "Spring," "The Lantern out of Doors"; in fact, argues Fr. Boyle, the theme of God's action in man permeates all of the poetry.

The third theme emphasizes the realization of God's presence in the universe. God is "lightning and love" (# 28) Whose grandeur "will flame out, like shining from shook foil" (# 31). It is Christ Who, in "The Lantern out of Doors," is man's "first, fast, last friend." In poem 36 "the fire that breaks from thee then, a billion / Times told lovelier, more dangerous, O my chevalier!" It is God Who, in "Pied Beauty," is responsible for the beauty of nature. In poem 38 "the azurous hung hills are his world-wielding shoulder / Majestic—as a stallion stalwart, very-violet-sweet!" God is both "mighty a master" and "a father and fond" in "Valley of the Elwy."

Granted that this matter will appear from time to time in other of Hopkins' poems, because each stage is part of a process of growth and not a hermetically sealed unit, we can conclude that the first group of the mature poems corresponds to the first stage of the threefold division of the spiritual life.

Before proceeding to the next stage, I should make a very necessary qualification. If part of the critic's function is to isolate themes, motifs, images, symbols, metrical schemes, and the like, so that he can evaluate them, he is liable to the charge that he is temporarily distorting the whole work of art. This is particularly true in Hopkins' case because the more one studies his poetry, the more one appreciates the integration of the parts, the more one understands the unity of Hopkins' view of the universe. God's grace, for example, is not a truncated gift appearing merely in poems x, y, and z. As I have attempted to show in the early poems and as Downes has shown in the later poems, *prayer* is not a word present in some of the poems; it is the form of the poetry. Faith, hope, and charity are not virtues appearing in a poem or two; they are the essence of each and every poem that affirms God's glory. Once God's love is felt in "God's Grandeur," it is not a fact to be catalogued and filed away; it is a fact that must constantly be felt, through man's striving toward spiritual perfection and through God's loving assistance.

The second stage is characterized by affective prayer, "that form of mental prayer in which the affection of the heart (and the will) have a much larger share than the considerations of the intellect" [21] and the subject of which is the mysteries of the Incarnation and the Redemption; acquisition of the theological and the cardinal (moral) virtues; and imitation of Christ.[22] Although this matter can be found in *The Wreck,* the second and third groups of Hopkins' later poetry move from the purgative way to the illuminative way. Poems such as "Peace," "Spelt from Sibyl's Leaves," "The Handsome Heart," "The Leaden Echo and the Golden Echo," "Tom's Garland," and fragment 113 treat of the acquisition of the virtues and the exercise of them in this life. Witness the lines, "He is patient. Patience fills / His crisp combs, and that comes those ways we know," in poem 70, the sestet to poem 71, fragment 117, and the lines in "Felix Randal," which treat of the virtue of charity, which sees all men as children of God:

> This seeing the sick endears them to us, us too it endears.
> My tongue had taught thee comfort, touch had quenched thy tears,
> Thy tears that touched my heart, child, Felix, poor Felix Randal.

The receiving of the Eucharist, the sacrament intimately associated with charity, is the subject of "The Bugler's First Communion." There is the simple prayer, "Divine charity, dear charity, / Fast you every, fast bind," for the bride and groom in "At the Wedding March."

The Incarnation with Its extension, the Redemption and

membership in the Mystical Body of Christ, is the matrix from which all of Hopkins' mature poetry originates, yet allusions to these mysteries become more explicit in "The Blessed Virgin compared," "The Soldier," fragment 116, and "Margaret Clitheroe." Poems 57 and 72 are brilliant examples of membership with Christ in the Mystical Body through imitation of Him. "Hope holds to Christ the mind's own mirror out / To take His lovely likeness more and more" (# 113). We think of the ending of the letter to Bridges, quoted earlier: "and the imitation of this [Christ's 'great sacrifice'] the root of all moral good in other men."

St. Ignatius concludes the exercises of the second week with the following: "For let each reflect that he will make progress in all spiritual matters just so far as he shall have divested himself of his self-love, self-will, and self-interest." The critical test of the spiritual life, the obstacle that man must try to overcome (since God initiates the mystical experience, if there is to be one), is that of total self-abnegation and complete humility, the "essential conditions and key-points in the spiritual life. For without them no higher perfection is possible, and when they are present all the rest follows easily enough." [23]

We can trace the struggle in Hopkins' later poetry between the assertion of the will contrary to God's will and the attempt to achieve complete self-abnegation and total humility. Starting with the lines, "This pride of prime's enjoyment / Take as for tool, not toy meant / And hold at Christ's employment" (# 48), the conflict gains momentum with "Ribblesdale"—"Ah, the heir / To his own selfbent so bound"—through "Spelt from Sibyl's Leaves" (a poetic translation of the Two Standards Exercise), "Carrion Comfort," the "terrible" sonnets, and the opening lines of poem 74. That we have no poems embodying the degree of the perfect, that the last line of poem 74 is a supplication for divine assistance, testify to the honesty and depth of the struggle.

Had Hopkins' career as a poet ended before the later poetry, he would be a minor figure. His contribution to religious poetry might be compared with the lush spirituality in the poetry of such contemporaries as Alice Meynell and Coventry Patmore or with the eccentric spirituality in the novels of Baron Corvo. But his greatness—in terms of the spiritual life—rests on his mature poems. Spiritual growth involves real suffering and real self-discipline. The exercitant does not normally pass rapidly through the stages to receive the mystical experience. He must constantly pray, purify, mortify, and try as best as he can to imitate Christ's example. Fortunately for us, Hopkins' poetry helps us to see just how ludicrous Stephen's purgation is in Chapter IV of the *Portrait*. Secondly, the effort to master the critical test is an agonizing one. In the very midst of the conflict in "Carrion Comfort" the speaker comes to the terrible discovery that he may be taking pride in it. In poem 74 the speaker must learn to subdue his human desire for recognition. What saves him, and the nun, is the knowledge that union with God far exceeds any goal that worldly desires can realize.

The poetry of Hopkins—and this is of paramount importance for the study of Eliot's poetry—is a poetry of purgation and illumination, a poetry of the first two stages, ways fraught with obstacles, primarily the assertion of the will—the sin of self-love, or pride—ways that are desperately painful, that involve suffering, penance, humility, and self-sacrifice, but ways that are made easier for man by Christ's "great sacrifice," by the presence of the Holy Ghost, by Mary's intercession, and by God's grace. They are ways in which with man's striving toward spiritual perfection the spiritual world crashes through his loneliness to engulf him in love. From an entry made during his 1883 Beaumont retreat, we know that Hopkins understood the meaning of this growth: "In meditating on the Crucifixion I saw how my asking to be raised to a higher degree of grace was asking also to be lifted on a higher cross." [24]

We have seen how the stages of the spiritual life can constitute the form and matter of a man's art. This is not unexpected, though, considering that the man is a priest, a poet "to whom the truths of the order of grace have become so second nature that they pervade his every thought as the soul pervades the body." [25] Turning to Joyce, we will learn that the fivefold, rather than the threefold, division is present, and, unlike Hopkins, to whom the spiritual life is "second nature," the novelist is *using* the progression as a framework against which we must judge Stephen.

III

James Joyce

Since there are many studies of the structure of *A Portrait of the Artist as a Young Man*,[1] it may be presumptuous to offer another one, but the novel is built upon the stages of the fivefold division of the spiritual life, with a difference—the order of the stages is reversed and the individual stages are inverted. Because of the lack of agreement about the meaning of the *Portrait*, the problem of the relationship between Joyce and Stephen, and the problem of Stephen as the artist, it will be necessary to approach the novel from a few directions to determine Joyce's intention.

Before discussing Joyce's use of the spiritual life, we will establish its presence. Since Miss Underhill considers the awakening a separate way, we will have to turn to her for a description of it. The mystic conversion in this stage, she tells us, "is of so actual a nature that in comparison the normal world of past perception seems but twilit at the best." She continues, by pointing out "that an actual sense of blinding radiance is a constant accompaniment of this state of consciousness."[2] On the fourth page of Chapter V of the

Portrait we read, "His thinking was a dusk of doubt and selfmistrust, lit up at moments by the lightnings of intuition, but lightnings of so clear a splendour that in those moments the world perished about his feet as if it had been fireconsumed. . . ." (180) The process of awakening is given its fullest treatment—the vision of the girl in Chapter IV will be commented upon later—in the section in Chapter V in which Stephen composes the verses, the section commencing, "Towards dawn he awoke. O what sweet music! His soul was all dewy wet" (221).

Investigating the account of St. Francis of Assisi's mystic conversion, Miss Underhill concludes:

> Here, then, is the first stage of conversion. The struggle between two discrepant ideals of life has attained its term. A sudden and apparently "irrational" impulse to some decisive act reaches the surface-consciousness from the seething deeps. The impulse is followed; and the swift emergence of the transcendental sense results. This "unwonted visitation" effects an abrupt and involuntary alteration in the subject's consciousness: whereby he literally "finds himself another man." He is as one who has slept and now awakes. The crystallization of this new, at first fluid apprehension of Reality in the form of vision and audition: the pointing of the moral, the direct application of truth to the awakened self, follow.[3]

Stephen's soul awakens "all dewy wet" from his vision in sleep. "The struggle" in his case is between serving God or serving his imagination. "The direct application of truth" is his decision to leave Ireland, to "go to encounter for the millionth time the reality of experience and to forge in the smithy of my soul the uncreated conscience of my race" (257), for he feels his soul "free and fancy free" (252). The "new and more real work" [4] which the awakened soul must perform Stephen outlines in his manifesto to Cranly

(251). Finally, he tries to describe the "slow and dark birth" of the soul to Davin, who replies, "—Too deep for me, Stevie. . . . But a man's country comes first. Ireland first, Stevie. You can be a poet or a mystic after" (207-208).

Several passages from the beginning of Chapter IV should suffice to establish the presence of the second stage of this division [5] (the first stage of the threefold division), the purgative way, or the degree of beginners: "his resolute piety," "devotional areas," "his penance," "he drove his soul daily through an increasing circle of works of supererogation," "his soul in devotion," "his sinful soul," "his soul was enriched with spiritual knowledge," "his soul took up again her burden of pieties, masses and prayers and sacraments and mortifications," "constant mortification to undo the sinful past," "His prayers and fasts," "His confession," and "He named it with humility and shame and repented of it once more" (150-156).

The illuminative way is distinguished by affective prayer rather than mental prayer, acquisition of the virtues, and imitation of Christ. Although Stephen's prayer toward the end of Chapter III (142) tends to be affective rather than discursive and he imagines himself to be acquiring virtue (149), it is well to follow the description given by Miss Underhill to this stage, her third one. It is a stage consisting of "the consciousness of the Absolute, or 'sense of the presence of God'" and "the illuminated vision of the world." The person in this stage, experiencing this "illuminated vision," is so conscious of God's love that he enjoys "'all creatures in God and God in all creatures.'" [6] On the way to confession Stephen speculates on souls in a state of grace. Even though the frowsy girls along the curbstones were not beautiful, "their souls were seen by God; and if their souls were in a state of grace they were radiant to see: and God loved them, seeing them" (144).

For Miss Underhill the person reaching this stage has

made genuine spiritual progress; he is more positive about his relation to God. Chapter III ends with Stephen's receiving Communion and rejoicing over his new life: "Another life! A life of grace and virtue and happiness! It was true. It was not a dream from which he would wake. The past was past" (150). The author of *Mysticism* goes on to show that the mystic at this stage is conscious that God's love floods the world, that he has entered a new spiritual universe, the essence of which is "the 'new life' of peaceful charity." Striding homeward after confession, "conscious of an invisible grace pervading and making light his limbs," Stephen is a new person who finds contentment in a plain breakfast and in the realization that life is "simple and beautiful . . . after all!" (149)

The fourth stage is the dark night of the soul, one between illumination and union.[7] Since St. John of the Cross is the outstanding authority on this stage, and, based on what immediately follows and what will be shown later, a source for the *Portrait*, we will read Chapter II against his famous exposition, the *Dark Night of the Soul*. In the first version of the *Portrait*, Stephen "descended among the hells of Swedenborg and abased himself in the gloom of Saint John of the Cross."[8] In the *Graces of Interior Prayer* Fr. Poulain devotes a chapter to the two nights of the Saint in order to "describe a state of prayer which forms the extreme borderland separating ordinary prayer from the mystic union, properly so called." The first night, the night of the senses, contains five elements: a habitual aridity in which there is no inclination for reasoning or imagining; a persistent memory of God; a painful and persistent need for a closer union with God; a conflict brought about by the natural opposition to a persistent action of grace; and the beginning of God's action in the soul, of which the recipient is unconscious. Under sufferings accompanying the first night, Fr. Poulain lists tedium, torment of distractions, thirst for a closer union with God, and groaning of human nature under this conflict with the sensitive appetite. After examining the second night, the night of the spirit, he concludes that both nights belong to the mystic state. The first night is characterized by a cessation of the sensible faculties; the second night, by a rising of the mind to a higher mode of operation, the outcome of which is mystical union.[9]

There are numerous passages in Chapter II that establish the presence of this stage: a dusk "obscured his mind"; "an intuition, a foreknowledge of the future came to him"; "A vague dissatisfaction grew up within him"; he has "visions"; "a voice within him" speaks to him; by brooding, he eliminates "all those elements which he deemed common and insignificant"; he is troubled by "unrest" and "restless moodiness"; "some power" divests him of his anger; the image of uncle Charles "had lately been fading out of memory"; his reveries "sweep across and abase his intellect"; his brain is "sick and powerless"; he is "beyond the limits of reality"; "The memory of his childhood suddenly grew dim"; and he thinks of himself as "passing out of existence" (66-96). The single most important line in this chapter is the following: "He felt some dark presence moving irresistibly upon him from the darkness, a presence subtle and murmurous as a flood filling him wholly with itself" (102).

In Book II, Chapter V, of the *Dark Night*, the Carmelite mystic answers the question, "Why is the Divine light (which, as we say, illumines and purges the soul from its ignorances) here called by the soul a dark night?" Most of this chapter of the *Portrait* is bathed in darkness: "dark avenger," "darkness of his soul," "surrounded by darkness," "darkwindowed house," "dark corner," "in the darkness," "in dark courses and eddies," "dark eyes," "in the dark," "darkening lands," "darkness and silence," "dark rosy light," "darkness of sleep," "dark orgiastic riot," "dark slimy streets," "dark presence," "from the darkness," "dark pressure," and "darker than the swoon of sin" (64-104). Finally, in Book II, Chapter XXI, of the *Dark Night*, St. John of the Cross explains that the soul disguises itself to protect itself, on its journey to God, from its enemies: the devil, the world, and the flesh. Chapter II has strange scenes involving disguises: the identities of Mabel Hunter (69) and the skull in the doorway (70), the confusion over Stephen and Josephine (70) and Bertie Tallon (76), the costumes and make-up of the boys in the play (87), and the transformation of Stephen during the play (88).

Our recognition of the fifth stage,[10] or at least an advance upon the fourth stage, depends on our reading of Chapter I. Because this chapter is very complex, we will have to establish another source for the novel which embodies the stages of the spiritual life.

In view of the evidence for Joyce's respect for Dante,[11] it is reasonable to expect closer parallels between the latter's writings and the *Portrait* than the inversions suggested by Tindall [12] and Barbara Seward's study of Joyce's use of the rose as symbol and the "opposition and kinship between Stephen's experience [his climactic vision at the end of Chapter IV] and Dante's [in the last four cantos of the *Paradiso*]," [13] although her findings will be incorporated later. There are two scenes, in addition to the one examined by Miss Seward, that are inversions of the *Vita Nuova* and the *Paradiso*.

Of the two scenes the second is the more obvious one, and since our acceptance of the first scene as based on Dante depends to a large extent on our willingness to see Joyce's specific use of Dante elsewhere, it is necessary to examine the second one first. However, now we will note the similarities only; we will save the inversions for later, in the correct chronological order of the *Portrait*. For Miss Seward the scene of creativity in Chapter V has an "inescapable analogy with Dante," [14] but where she sees it in relation to the *Paradiso,* I accept Stephen's testimony in *Stephen Hero* that the *Vita Nuova* provides the inspiration for his "scattered love-verses." [15] The material of the earlier version carried over to the *Portrait* is presented more elliptically and obliquely. If the *Vita Nuova* is to appear in the *Portrait,* we should expect to find it woven into the novel, not talked about directly by Stephen.

In the *Vita Nuova* Dante and Beatrice first meet when he is nine, she eight (II). Nine years later they meet again, which meeting results in the sonnet, "To every captive soul and gentle heart" (III). In the *Portrait* Stephen "had written verses for her again after ten years. . . . Ten years from that wisdom of children to his folly" (226).

In the interim "her image . . . continually abode with" Dante (II). In the novel "distorted reflections of her image started from his memory": the flower girl, the kitchengirl, the girl who laughed when he stumbled, and the girl from Jacob's biscuit factory (224-225).

At their first meeting Beatrice is dressed in crimson (II); at the second, white (III). In the *Portrait* Emma's "strange wilful heart" is a white flame which deepens to "a rose and ardent light" (221-222).

When Beatrice salutes Dante (the second meeting), "such sweetness possessed me that as one drunken I departed from all people" (III); at the beginning of the scene of creativity, which occurs ten years after an earlier meeting, Stephen "lay still, as if his soul lay amid cool waters, conscious of faint sweet music" (221).

Following their meeting Dante falls asleep and experiences a vision in which Beatrice, naked, appears to him. The lord of love, who accompanies her, has Dante's flaming heart in his hand, which he forces her to eat. After awakening, Dante ponders the meaning of the vision and composes the sonnet (III). This scene in the novel opens with Stephen's awakening from a dream or vision (221). It is during the final inspiration that Emma's "nakedness yielded to him" (227). The rays from her wilful heart "burned up the world, consumed the hearts of men and angels" (222).

In Dante's vision the lord of love ascends to heaven with Beatrice in his arms (III). Stephen imagines "a rose-way from where he lay upwards to heaven all strewn with scarlet flowers" (226).

As a result of thinking of her, Dante becomes "frail and weak" (IV); Stephen is wearied as a result of composing the villanelle to Emma (226).

From the beginning, Dante confesses, "Love held lordship over my soul" (II). However Stephen "might revile and mock her image, his anger was also a form of homage" (225).

The author of the *Vita Nuova* is advised by the lord of love to adorn his verses with music (XII). In his reverie Stephen, seated at the piano, sings to Emma (223).

Beholding Beatrice at the gathering of ladies honoring the gentlewoman to be married, Dante has his senses so destroyed that he is transformed (XIV). In Stephen's memory Emma, at the gathering, dances toward him, a transformed person, a monk (223-224).

Finally, the vision of Beatrice causes Dante to begin "to repent grievously" of his base desire (XL). For one brief moment Stephen begins "to feel that he had wronged her" (227).

In summary we find the following parallels: both Dante and Stephen meet the females when they are children; carry their images with them; experience visions in their sleep in which the females, naked, appear to them; experience awakenings; compose verses approximately ten years after the meetings; are weakened or wearied; consider themselves subjects of the females; are transformed; and repent of wrongs done to the females. The following elements are also present, although altered in the novel: the colors white and red, associated with the females; sweetness; burning hearts; passages to heaven; and music to accompany their verses. On the basis of these parallels and Stephen's admission in *Stephen Hero,* I think a valid conclusion is that the scene of creativity in the *Portrait* is based on Dante's experience in the *Vita Nuova.*

If we will accept this work as the source for this scene, the second one, then we should re-examine the role of Dante in the opening of the novel, the first scene. In Canto XIX of the *Paradiso,* the eagle of justice—composed of eagles, souls of the just—informs Dante that human sight is limited (58-66). In Canto XXI the spirit of Peter Damiani reminds him that he " 'hast the hearing, as the sight, of mortals, / ... wherefore here is no song / for that same reason for which Beatrice hath not smiled' " (61-63). In the next canto Dante's human sight prevents him from seeing the summit of Jacob's ladder, and Beatrice cautions him, " 'Thou art so nigh to the supreme weal / ... that thou shouldst have thine eyes / clear and keen' " (124-126). In Canto XXIII Dante is momentarily blinded by the light of Christ (28-33); by the final canto his sight is completely purged so that he can receive the mystical experience (49-63).

On the second page of the novel, the injunction, "Dante said:—O, if not, the eagles will come and pull out his eyes—," may refer to the message of the eagle, or the eagles, in Cantos XIX and XX. Indeed, since the entire movement of the *Commedia* is that of the purgation of human faculties, senses, interests, desires, and attachments—in a sense, a pulling out of the eyes—so that Dante can progress to the mystical experience at the end of the *Paradiso,* this line by Joyce may be a capsule pinpointing of the work against which the *Portrait* should be read. Further, in Cantos XXIV-XXVI, which I hope to show will explain the Christmas dinner scene, Dante is blinded by the light of St. John the Evangelist, one of whose symbols is the eagle. At least, based on the relation between the *Vita Nuova* and the scene of creativity, we should consider the possibility that certain material of the *Commedia* may be present.

Stanislaus Joyce identifies the source of Dante Riordan as Mrs. Conway, and while so doing, indicates which of her traits Joyce includes in the *Portrait*. He does not, however, give corresponding facts for every passage. According to him Mrs. Conway taught James "some elementary arithmetic and geography."[16] In the *Portrait* "Dante knew a lot of things. She had taught him where the Mozambique Channel was and what was the longest river in America and what was the name of the highest mountain in the moon" (10-11), the last part of which is a rather odd geography lesson, even for a boy, but it may allude to the cosmography of the *Commedia*. In the novel Dante suffers from "heartburn" (11), which forces one to recall Dante's vision in the *Vita Nuova*, in which Beatrice eats his burning heart. The fact that Dante Alighieri depicts Beatrice as dressed in crimson in the *Vita Nuova* and green in the *Purgatorio* adds a symbolic dimension to the maroon and green brushes Dante Riordan carries. Then, too, the first time Stephen thinks about God, he looks "wearily at the green round earth in the middle of the maroon clouds" (16).

Of course, the *Commedia* is inverted in the novel. On the simplest level the inversion occurs in the names. Dante's surname is the first three letters of *Dante* and the last two letters of *Alighieri*, transposed. E. C. are the last two letters of *Beatrice*, transposed. The main dish at the Christmas dinner, turkey, is described as "the real Ally Daly" (31), the first two letters of each word forming a play on *Dante Alighieri*, transposed. Note that two of the distorted reflections of Emma's image are the flower girl and the girl from Jacob's biscuit factory. (In Canto XXII of the *Paradiso*, Beatrice is Dante's guide by Jacob's ladder.)

Admittedly, this is a slender argument, but it is based

on the following considerations: it does not deny that Mrs. Conway is a source for Dante Riordan and John Kelly is a source for John Casey; it does raise these characters and the crucial scene about to be examined, the Christmas dinner scene, to the level of a fusion of the symbolic and the naturalistic. Recent scholarship discovers a much larger symbolic element with the naturalistic in the novel than Harry Levin does.[17] My argument pays attention to names; it assumes that nothing in Joyce is irrelevant, not even Dante's "heartburn"; and it explains Stephen's desire early in the novel to find a green rose: "But you could not have a green rose. But perhaps somewhere in the world you could" (12). In the *Purgatorio* Beatrice appears "within a cloud of flowers ... under a green mantle" (XXX.28-33). It also provides a link with Stephen's quest for Mercedes. As the sweetheart of Edmond Dantes in *The Count of Monte Cristo*, which Stephen reads (64), she is a counterpart to Beatrice.

Canto XXIV of the *Paradiso* opens with Beatrice's appeal to the saints to allow Dante to partake of the divine feast, Christ the Lamb. They "'drink ever of the fountain,'" which is Christ (1-9). At the opening of the Christmas dinner scene in the *Portrait*, Simon and John start the festivities with a drink, and drinks are manufactured by their friend, "Christopher," or "Christy" (30), who is mentioned one other time in the novel. After the turkey has been carved and partially distributed to the guests, Simon Dedalus comments that "Christy" is "nearly lopsided now with roguery" (31).

Following Beatrice's appeal the three saints—(Simon) Peter, James, and John—one by one leave the atmosphere of the starry heavens to question Dante (XXIV-XXV). Before Simon pours the drinks, he casually says to John Casey, "O, well now, we got a good breath of ozone round the Head to-day. Ay, bedad" (28).

As the receiver of the keys, (Simon) Peter is traditionally looked upon as the gatekeeper of Heaven. Twice during this scene Stephen sees and hears "the hotel keeper" (30) in Simon's face and voice. This is not one of the occupations in the list later offered by him to Cranly (245).

In Cantos XXIV-XXVI (Simon) Peter tests Dante on faith; James, on hope; and John, on charity. In the *Portrait* John Casey questions Dante on an extension of charity: "—And can we not love our country then?" (39) Throughout the scene Dante is on the defensive: "God and morality and religion come first" (40).

A careful examination of John Casey, the counterpart to St. John the Evangelist, will reveal Joyce's method. Rev. xvii contains the image of the great harlot sitting upon a scarlet-colored beast, full of names of blasphemy, having seven heads and ten horns. In Canto XIX of the *Inferno,* Dante, who with Virgil descends to speak to the simoniacs, refers to her when he accuses the shade of Pope Nicholas III of deifying "gold and silver" (106-114). The spiritually corrosive effect of simony is one of Joyce's major themes; in Chapter IV Stephen's desire to know the sin of Simon Magus is one reason he flirts with the idea of becoming a priest. In the *Portrait* John Casey is described as silver-throated: "He smiled to think how the silvery noise which Mr. Casey used to make had deceived him. And when he had tried to open Mr. Casey's hand to see if the purse of silver was hidden there ..." (28), for which neither Stanislaus nor Ellmann gives an explanation. Just as Simon is inverted to a "hotel keeper" and Christ's *Noli me tangere* (a motif in Chapter V), from John xx.17, is inverted to "*Touch them not,* says Christ, *for they are the apple of My eye*" (39), by Dante Riordan, so, too, is St. John the Evangelist ironically inverted because the implication of the silver throat is that St. John, the author of Revelation and attacker of avarice, is John Casey at the Christmas banquet and himself guilty of simony. The inversions continue throughout this scene. Along with the allegorical meaning of Dante's test in Cantos XXIV-XXVI, there is a tradition that at one time he was suspected of heresy and these cantos may be the proof that his views were orthodox, yet for one moment at the dinner, Dante reverses the roles by yelling "Blasphemer!" (40) at John Casey.

Dante Alighieri is blinded by John; his sight is not restored until he completes his examination on love (XXV-XXVI). During the dinner Mrs. Dedalus reminds her husband that Dante does not have any sauce. His reply seems more than a cliché: "Mrs. Riordan, pity the poor blind" (32). Later in the scene, provoked by Dante, John recounts how one day in Arklow he spit in the eye of "a drunken old harridan," who cried out, "—*O Jesus, Mary and Joseph! . . . I'm blinded! I'm blinded and drownded! . . . I'm blinded entirely*" (37-38). At the height of the violence, Dante almost spits in his face (40).

The argument revolves around Parnell, a "dead king" (41) for John Casey, a false king for Dante—perhaps an allusion to the ending of Canto XIX, where the eagle denounces false kings. Dante leaves, screaming, "—Devil out of hell! We won! We crushed him to death! Fiend!" (41) never to reappear in the novel.

Here, again, my reading offers a satisfactory explanation for passages that are otherwise irrelevant or insignificant. Read as a purely naturalistic scene, interesting as it is, there is no significance to Christopher, Simon as a hotel keeper, John's silver throat, blindness, and Dante's exit. If we decide that the scene is a fusion of the naturalistic and the symbolic, then Dante's exit symbolizes the rejection in Stephen's world of Dante Alighieri's vision of man's spiritual ascent: "—O, he'll remember all this when he grows up, said Dante hotly—the language he heard against God and religion and priests in his own home" (35). The symbolic exit of Dante will explain an important scene in Chapter II, which if read as purely naturalistic, can at most indicate Stephen's disdain for authority. In Chapter II he recalls how "on a certain Tuesday" Mr. Tate, the English master, accused him of heresy for writing in an essay that the soul is "*without a possibility of ever approaching nearer*" its Creator. Stephen submits by explaining that he meant "*ever reaching*" its Creator (81).

The dismissal of Dante by the Dedalus elders is not final. It remains for Stephen to articulate his rejection of Dante Alighieri's vision, in addition to the comic inversions of Chapter I, for the meaning of this chapter is clear. In Stephen's world Dante Alighieri is Dante Riordan, a bigoted defender of the Irish priesthood, and his *Commedia*, a secular comedy. Miss Seward has shown that the vision of the girl in Chapter IV is Dante's ultimate vision inverted: Stephen's experience "being inspired by primarily sensual feelings, the crimson rose represents his supreme affirmation of the 'wonder of mortal beauty,' in direct contrast to Dante's white rose of spiritual beauty." [18] Stephen's vision, then, is to be a secular one. The disparity between Dante's vision and Stephen's, between Dante's ecstasy and Stephen's, between what Stephen experiences and what Joyce ironically underscores is all summed up in the line, "—Heavenly God! cried Stephen's soul, in an outburst of profane joy" (176).

First there is the expulsion of Dante, then the inversion of his vision, and then the awakening—for good reason: Stephen's vision is his beginning. The *Vita Nuova* concludes with the germ of the *Commedia*: Dante will convert the earthly experience with Beatrice into a spiritual one. His "new life" is a dawning recognition that his goal is the spiritual world and the journey of the *Commedia*. Beatrice communicates beatitude to him in the *Vita Nuova*, but in the final three cantos of the *Paradiso* she takes her rightful place, leaving him free to receive the mystical experience. His "new life" is a prelude to the true life of the soul.

Stephen's "new life" is the life of art, of creativity. The vision of Emma, which is erotic, leads him, not to an interior reforming of his spiritual life in any kind of orthodox sense and not to a spiritual realm that crashes through the natural such as is found in Hopkins' poetry, but to a life of art. He is to be, not a priest of God, but "a priest of the eternal imagination" (225), dedicated to forging "in the smithy of my soul the uncreated conscience of my race" (257), not to making his soul worthy of God's grace and not to praying for God's assistance in making His glory known to men, as Dante does, in the *Paradiso* (XXXIII.67-75). It is not until Stephen consciously—much of the visions of the girl on the beach and of Emma is unconscious—rejects "the spiritual-heroic refrigerating apparatus, invented and patented in all countries by Dante Alighieri" (256) that the novel comes full circle, that Stephen invokes the assistance of another "old father, old artificer" (257).

I think it safe to state that one of Joyce's early "gods," [19] Dante, does appear in the *Portrait* but put to a special Joycean use. In fact, a close reading of Stephen's spiritual development, Dante's reversed and inverted, gives us a tremendous insight into Joyce's intention in the novel.

Chapter I, then, is the possibility of the fifth stage—infused contemplation, or the degree of the perfect, or the unitive way—rejected.

Now that it has been demonstrated that the stages of the fivefold division are present, in reverse order, and that the fifth stage is inverted, the next step will be to prove that the other four stages are inverted. According to St. John of the Cross in the *Dark Night,* the reason for the cessation of the faculties of understanding, will, and memory is union of the soul with God (I.i). For Stephen the culmination of the cessation is surrender to his sensual nature, in the brothel scene. That is, he succumbs to the temptations to the senses, analyzed by the Saint in Book I, Chapter XIV.

In Book I, Chapter XI, the Carmelite mystic describes the progress of the soul's yearning for God. To summarize Stephen's progress, we must return to an important passage in Chapter II, the one in which he longs "to meet in the real world the unsubstantial image which his soul so constantly beheld." He knows that "they would meet quietly as if they had known each other and had made their tryst, perhaps at one of the gates or in some more secret place. They would be alone, surrounded by darkness and silence; and in that moment of supreme tenderness he would be transfigured" (66-67). St. John of the Cross explains what the gate is: "The strait gate is this night of the sense, and the soul detaches itself from sense and strips itself thereof that it may enter by this gate, and establishes itself in faith, which is a stranger to all sense, so that afterwards it may journey by the narrow way, which is the other night—that of the spirit—and this the soul afterwards enters in order to journey to God in pure faith, which is the means whereby the soul is united to God. By this road, since it is so narrow, dark and terrible. . . ." (I.xi) Stephen progresses from the "darkness of his soul" (66) to "a cold and cruel and loveless lust" (98) to an inverted infused contemplation. He suffers the "agony of its penetration" (102).

The most damning instance is the inversion of the final three stanzas (which describe the mystical marriage) of the Carmelite mystic's poem, "En una Noche Oscura," the first two stanzas of which are explicated in the *Ascent of Mount Carmel* and the *Dark Night of the Soul,*

> Upon my flowery breast,
> Kept wholly for himself alone,
> There he stayed sleeping, and I caressed him,
> And the fanning of the cedars made a breeze.
>
> The breeze blew from the turret
> As I parted his locks;

With his gentle hand he wounded my neck
And caused all my senses to be suspended.

I remained, lost in oblivion;
My face I reclined on the Beloved.
All ceased and I abandoned myself,
Leaving my cares forgotten among the lilies,

in the scene in Chapter II in which Stephen realizes "the unsubstantial image." In the room with the prostitute, he "all but burst into hysterical weeping. Tears of joy and relief shone in his delighted eyes and his lips parted though they would not speak. . . . He wanted to be held firmly in her arms, to be caressed slowly, slowly, slowly." The final paragraph reads:

> With a sudden movement she bowed his head and joined her lips to his and he read the meaning of her movements in her frank uplifted eyes. It was too much for him. He closed his eyes, surrendering himself to her, body and mind, conscious of nothing in the world but the dark pressure of her softly parting lips. They pressed upon his brain as upon his lips as though they were the vehicle of a vague speech; and between them he felt an unknown and timid pressure, darker than the swoon of sin, soften than sound or odour (103-104).

I prefer not to investigate at this point the inversions of stages two and three; this will be done later. We can finish this section, though, by noting how Joyce's first stage differs from the orthodox one, in which the soul awakens to the divine Reality of God. Stephen awakens to the life of the artist, who is "like the God of creation" (219).[20]

The next step is to study Joyce's use of another source which embodies the stages of the spiritual life, St. Augustine's *Confessions*, "an archetype for the *Portrait*."[21] First, we will see how closely Chapter I of the novel parallels Book I of this work. St. Augustine's chronological autobiography begins with infancy; Stephen's biography, with infancy. As an infant the Saint "did reprehensible things." Mrs. Dedalus promises that "Stephen will apologize" for whatever he has done wrong. Augustine ponders the meaning of words as Stephen does. Both are punished, unjustly they think, in school; both punishments are treated lightly by their parents. As children both suffer temporary stomach ailments; the former is very close to death; the latter is disturbed by images of the dead marshal, the dead rats, and the dead Parnell. The two boys, promising students, are physically weak. Both desire adulation.

Augustine's studies are interrupted because of his father's financial difficulties, and he spends a year of idleness at home (II.iii). Because of Simon Dedalus' financial trouble, Stephen does not return to Clongowes, the family moves, and he becomes acquainted with Dublin (65-68). Book II of the *Confessions* commences the psychological analysis of its author's early life of concupiscence: "Where was I in that sixteenth year of my body's age, and how long was I exiled from the joys of your house? Then it was that the madness of lust, licensed by human shamelessness but forbidden by your laws, took me completely under its scepter, and I clutched it with both hands" (II.ii). In Chapter II Stephen wanders "up and down the dark slimy streets" (102) searching for an outlet for his lust. The former confesses to acknowledging pretended sins as well as real ones (II.iii). In Chapter III we discover that the latter's sins are of "thought and deed; his monstrous dreams, peopled by apelike creatures and by harlots with gleaming jewel eyes; the foul long letters he had written in the joy of guilty confession. . . ." (119)

With companions Augustine steals from a pear tree in a garden (II.iv,viii); Stephen, with Aubrey Mills, joins a gang of adventurers who "make forays into the gardens of old maids" (65). Patricius is not especially interested in his son's spiritual development (II.iii). Simon, who calls Stephen "an impudent thief," is more concerned about his getting ahead in the world than about his spiritual welfare (73-74). "The theater enraptured me," confesses St. Augustine, because he could experience the emotions of the performers (III.ii). It is during his participation in the school play that Stephen experiences a transformation, that he shares the mirth of the others (88).

Augustine is confused by metaphysical and theological questions (III.vii); Stephen, too, engages in such subtleties (109-110). Both practice their hands at poetry (III.vii; 72-73). Both win contests (IV.iii; 99). Both are interested in aesthetics, and both theories receive comments, the Saint's in a short passage (IV.xv), Stephen's at length to Lynch (208-219).

Finally, there is the area of Manicheism. During his commitment to Manicheism Augustine is confronted with the problem of evil (III.vii). In Book V, Chapter X, he admits that at this time in his life he "postulated two masses opposed to one another, each of them infinite, but the evil one on a narrower scale, the good one larger. From this pestilential beginning other blasphemies pursued me." The force with which Stephen believes in the reality of the dark presence, the inverted infused contemplation, in Chapter II, and his belief in the power of evil as of good (106-107) place him dangerously near to the Manichean heresy. As Manicheans Augustine and others "were seduced and we seduced others, deceived and deceiving by various desires" (IV.i). Stephen "wanted to sin with another of his kind, to force another being to sin with him and to exult with her in sin" (102).

We may look now at Joyce's inversions. St. Augustine leaves no doubt that his confessions are not merely those

of sins but those of faith and praise as well. The *Confessions*
opens with an extended declaration of faith and praise. The
first time Stephen thinks about God, he becomes very tired
(16). The Saint speculates on God's immensity and man's
relation to Him (I.iii-v); Stephen does, also, but with a
difference, for the thought of sin "thrilled him" (47).

The important use of the *Confessions* is found in Chapter V, the chapter in which Stephen admits to Cranly that
he has confessed to him (251). After the chronological and
spiritual autobiography of the first nine books, St. Augustine
turns his attention to disquisitions on memory, time and
eternity, form and matter, and creation in Books X, XI, XII,
and XIII. Chapter V of the *Portrait* opens with Stephen
seated at the table "staring into the dark pool of the jar.
The yellow dripping had been scooped out like a boghole
and the pool under it brought back to his memory the dark
turfcoloured water of the bath in Clongowes" (177).[22] In
Book X of the *Confessions* a frequent image for the recesses
of the mind is cave or cavern, but where the author desires
to pass beyond in his quest for self-knowledge and knowledge of God, Stephen is reluctant to know himself: "Through
this image he had a glimpse of a strange dark cavern of
speculation but at once turned away from it, feeling that it
was not yet the hour to enter it" (182).

Book XI is the examination of time and eternity. On
the second page of this chapter, Stephen asks, "—How much
is the clock fast now?" (178) Passing the consumptive man,[23]
he begins to think about the time (180-181). As an illustra-
tion of his thesis that time is an activity of the mind, a mental
synthesis, St. Augustine offers the following:

> I am about to recite a psalm that I know. Before I begin,
> my expectation extends over the entire psalm. Once I have
> begun, my memory extends over as much of it as I shall
> separate off and assign to the past. The life of this action

59

of mine is distended into memory by reason of the part
I have spoken and into forethought by reason of the part
I am about to speak. But attention is actually present and
that which was to be is borne along by it so as to become
past. The more this is done and done again, so much the
more is memory lengthened by a shortening of expectation,
until the entire expectation is exhausted. When this is done
the whole action is completed and passes into memory
(XI.xxviii).

We read in Chapter V that Stephen's

> morning walk across the city had begun, and he foreknew
> that as he passed the sloblands of Fairview he would think
> of the cloistral silverveined prose of Newman; that as he
> walked along the North Strand Road, glancing idly at the
> windows of the provision shops, he would recall the dark
> humour of Guido Cavalcanti and smile; that as he went by
> Baird's stonecutting works in Talbot Place the spirit of Ibsen
> would blow through him like a keen wind, a spirit of way-
> ward boyish beauty.... (179)

The final two books of the *Confessions* are concerned with
form and matter and creation. Chapter V contains Stephen's
definition of art (211) and his comparison of the artist and
God (219), which should be contrasted with a passage in
Book XI, Chapter V, where St. Augustine eloquently explains how the artist is dependent upon God. At the time
the Saint wrote a treatise on aesthetics, "On the Beautiful
and the Fitting," he was in error (IV.xv). It is later that he
comes to understand the essence of beauty, defined in the
passage beginning, "Too late have I loved you, O Beauty
so ancient and so new, too late have I loved you! Behold,
you were within me, while I was outside" (X.xxvii). But
where St. Augustine's "heart is restless until it rests" in God,
Stephen is arrested within himself.

We have seen how Chapter II culminates in an inversion of the *Dark Night* and Chapter V concludes with an articulated rejection of Dante. The *Confessions* is also inverted at the ending of Chapter V. For April 6 he enters in his diary the following: "Certainly she remembers the past. Lynch says all women do. Then she remembers the time of her childhood—and mine, if I was ever a child. The past is consumed in the present and the present is living only because it brings forth the future" (255), which alludes to passages in the disquisition on time and eternity such as the following: "But how is the future, which as yet does not exist, diminished or consumed, or how does the past, which no longer exists, increase, unless there are three things in the mind, which does all this?" (XI.xxviii) The inversion consists in the fact that Stephen's inquiry into time and memory is incomplete, that he does not pass beyond memory, that he does not penetrate the meaning of time, as the Saint does, to arrive at the ending of the *Confessions*, where he praises God and His works (XIII.xxxiii). The diary entries which terminate the novel—each one prefaced by a date, the totality of which deflates Stephen's soaring mission [24]—and his definition of history in *Ulysses*, "a nightmare from which I am trying to awake," testify to his inability to penetrate the meaning of time and eternity. Finally, Stephen's spiritual biography concludes with praise for another "old father, old artificer" (257).

At this point let us review our finds. The stages are reversed: the novel opens with the fifth stage and proceeds through the first. In addition, the individual stages are inverted: the mystical experience is rejected, the dark night leads to a brothel, and Stephen awakens to the life of the artist. The inversions of stages two and three will be examined shortly.

The critical test of the spiritual life is that of complete humility and total self-abnegation. Hopkins, the commenta-

tors referred to in the previous chapter, the sources for the
Portrait, St. Paul (allusions to his writings will be noted
later), St. Thomas (whom Stephen professes to know via a
Synopsis) are all in agreement that the chief obstacle to
spiritual growth is pride. Two "fatal spiritual maladies,"
writes Fr. Garrigou-Lagrange, are "pride and spiritual
sloth." [25] Spiritual sloth, or *acedia* (*accidie*), is a disgust at
the thought of the effort required for spiritual growth. It
can result in a denial of grace because the grace reminds
the person of his spiritual obligations.[26] Bearing in mind the
relation of pride, which prevents one from truly knowing
himself, and self-knowledge is a characteristic of the beginning stage of the ascent toward knowledge and love of God;
humility, which overcomes pride; charity, which is love of
God and His creatures; and *acedia,* which is overcome by
charity and true devotion of the will, we will resume with
the study of the *Portrait,* pausing to examine the inversions
of Chapters III and IV, stages three and two.

The first time the word *God* appears in the novel, and
it appears fourteen times in this passage, Stephen's reaction
exhibits both spiritual maladies: "It made him very tired to
think that way. It made him feel his head very big. He
turned over the flyleaf and looked wearily at the green round
earth in the middle of the maroon clouds" (16). Both pride
("head very big") and sloth ("wearily") are the keys to his
character. When he decides to inform the rector that he has
been wrongly punished, he compares himself to "the great
men" in history whose nobility was recognized by "the senate
and the Roman people" (54-55). After the interview he is
"happy and free; but he would not be anyway proud with
Father Dolan" (60). Beginning with Chapter II instances
of sloth and pride increase in frequency. Stephen cannot
share his uncle's piety (62), and his prayer is "addressed
neither to God nor saint" (90). On three different occasions
he is described as being "weary"; on two of these occasions

his father is the cause. There are numerous examples of his growing alienation, the result of his pride.[27] In Chapter III he is described as being "weary" three times; twice we are told "pride" is the cause of his spiritual predicament.

In this chapter and the next one St. John of the Cross is again a source. In the *Dark Night of the Soul*, Book I, Chapters II-VII, he discusses the imperfections of beginners in terms of the seven deadly sins.[28] Stephen also applies these sins to himself, elsewhere (109).[29] The first, of course, is pride. Joyce's ironic treatment of Stephen's pride and false humility begins slowly with passages such as "Ah yes, he would still be spared; he would repent in his heart and be forgiven; and then those above, those in heaven, would see what he would do to make up for the past: a whole life, every hour of life. Only wait" (129) and "—Sorry! Sorry! O sorry!" (147), increases in intensity with passages such as "his prayers ascended to heaven from his purified heart like perfume streaming upwards from a heart of white rose" (149) and the scene with him seated by the fire in the kitchen (149), until it reaches devastating proportions in passages such as the one in which he stores up prayers for the souls in purgatory (150-151) and the one in which he feels "his soul in devotion pressing like fingers the keyboard of a great cash register" (151). The Carmelite mystic continues with his listing of the effects of pride, one of which is a condemnation of more devout persons. Worshippers at church sicken Stephen (107), and his classmates are like cattle to him (129). Joyce spells out Stephen's problem: "To merge his life in the common tide of other lives was harder for him than any fasting or prayer. . . ." (155) Shame in confessing is also an effect of pride for the Saint as it is for Stephen (143,146).

Under avarice the Saint warns the beginner against focusing his attention on objects such as rosaries and books rather than on spiritual growth. Stephen says his rosary as he walks through the streets (151) and enjoys books of spiritual counsel (150-155). Under luxury St. John of the Cross explains that when there comes to exercitants "some spiritual consolation or delight in prayer, the spirit of luxury is with them immediately, inebriating and delighting their sensual nature in such manner that they are, as it were, plunged into the enjoyment and pleasure of this sin." Stephen luxuriates in the realization that by an act of will he can continue his purgative stage or plunge himself into sin again (155-156).

For the fourth, wrath, the Saint writes that when beginners lose enjoyment in spiritual growth, they become irritated over trivial matters. About Stephen we are told that he is easily irritated, especially by his mother's sneezing (154-155). Further, the Saint warns against being impatient that the imperfections are not quickly removed, one of the more distressing aspects of Stephen's purgation (156). The Carmelite mystic next discusses the sin of gluttony, the beginner's attempt to accomplish more than his frailty can bear. Stephen's attempts to mortify his smell and touch are truly comic (154).

Since envy is antithetical to charity, it will be enough to recall Stephen's contempt for worshippers at church. The seventh one, sloth, has been indicated frequently, although it should be noted that, according to St. John of the Cross, many a beginner has difficulty submitting his will to God's will because he expects God to will what he wills. Stephen, too, has difficulty because he believes "God was obliged to give" him grace (156).

The author of the *Dark Night* concludes each chapter with a reminder that the mystical purgation removes any traces of these imperfections, preparing the soul for infused contemplation. Not only does Joyce conclude Stephen's purgative stage with a final irony, "—I have amended my life, have I not? he asked himself" (157), but since the dark night of the soul stage has already taken place in Chapter II and since there it is inverted to climax in a brothel, Stephen's spiritual isolation is, by the middle of Chapter IV, almost complete.

Starting with the end of Chapter III and continuing through Chapter IV, examples of Stephen's sloth and pride multiply. For him the voice of the priest hearing his confession (148) and those of his brothers and sisters are "weary" (168).[30] His reaction to the suggestion that he may have the call to the priesthood is motivated by pride (162-163), in a passage that is an inversion of St. Paul's clarification of the priest's role.[31] In Chapter V he sees sloth and weariness in the city (180), the statue (183), the images of kings (254), and the lover (255). He is described as being "weary" in his search for beauty (180), in class (197), during and after the act of creativity (223-226), and on the steps of the library (228-229). There are references to the "pride of his youth" (179), "his monkish pride" (180), his "pride of silence" (180), and "his baffled pride" (225). He rejects the flower girl (187), and the woman woos Davin, not him (185-186). There is the evidence of MacCann's comment (203), MacAlister's caustic remark (203), Davin's insight (207), Cranly's hostility, Lynch's mockery, Stephen's refusal to serve (243), his failure to recognize the humanity of Rosie (249), his judgment on the Irish (254), and his mother's farewell (257).

There is another allusion to St. Paul in a passage in Chapter III, the one in which he meets "his sins face to face" (140).[32] Tindall is undoubtedly correct in his examination of the scene in which Stephen, on the steps of the library, considers the meaning of the birds.[33] Their flight, their association with Agrippa, Swedenborg, and Thoth symbolize for him the direction he must take: "and he felt that the augury he had sought in the wheeling darting birds and in the pale space of sky above him had come forth from his heart like a bird from a turret, quietly and swiftly" (230).

However, since there are two allusions to the writings of St. Paul and since St. Augustine is a source for the *Portrait*, possibly we are to see in this scene another instance of Stephen's pride. Possibly this scene also alludes to St. Paul's condemnation of those who "exchanged the glory of the incorruptible God for an image made like corruptible man and to birds and four-footed beasts and creeping things" (Rom. i.18-25) and to St. Augustine's assimilation of this passage in Book V, Chapter III, of the *Confessions*, beginning, "Out of an impious pride they fall back from you and suffer an eclipse of your light. . . . Nor do they slay their own prideful boasts, which are like the fouls of the air. . . ." What is wrong with Stephen is not that he possesses a dedication to his art, but that, like Icarus, he suffers from pride.

How, then, are we to read the novel? How are we to answer the questions raised by Booth? [34] Is it possible to reconcile interpretations as divergent as, at one extreme, Miss Gordon's and, at the other, Morse's and Daiches'? [35] We must eliminate the distortion caused by the establishment of the presence of the stages. Putting them back into proper perspective, we realize that they do not constitute the sole concern of the novel: for example, stage three takes up only a few pages at the end of Chapter III; stage two, only a few pages at the beginning of Chapter IV. Yet their presence, in reversed and inverted order, helps to explain why a young man dedicated to art is spiritually isolated not only from those persons antagonistic to him or to art but also from those sympathetic as well. Structure is one of the techniques leading to discovery.

If Stephen were the mature artist at the end of the *Portrait*, it would be interesting to speculate on the following: in a society hostile to art and the artist, an environment that has lost its heritage, a Dublin where the traditional cultural patterns and values are broken and submerged under a welter of spiritless Church, university, home, family, community, the spiritual development of the artist-to-be, of necessity, must be different. Not only must he create the art that will reorient and save mankind, he must first create a new spiritual life for himself, a spiritual life that is the reverse of the orthodox one. In a sense, the artist-to-be must perform a Black Mass. But despite the awakening scene, which has a validity, the facts of the *Portrait* and *Ulysses* do not support this hypothesis, for if we argue it, we are left with the conclusion that following his reversed, inverted spiritual development, the artist as a young man is then incapable of creating art. I agree with Poss, when he writes that readers make a mistake expecting Stephen to create a great work,[36] but we cannot ignore Joyce's constant deflation of Stephen throughout the novel, in passages such as the one in which his ecstatic flight is punctured by the shout, "—Oh, Cripes, I'm drownded!" (173) and we cannot ignore the opening of *Ulysses*, where Stephen is incapable of creating art. Significantly, both spiritual maladies are present in his first appearance: on the first page Stephen looks "coldly" at Buck and follows him "wearily"; on the next page he "suffers" Buck to pull out his handkerchief.

At the same time, however, that his spiritual development is taking place, he is developing as an artist-to-be. To deny this is to deny the epiphany in Chapter IV, the validity of the awakening scene, the composition of the villanelle, his sense of dedication, his groping with aesthetics, the imagery of the end of Chapter IV and of Chapter V, his growing awareness of the possibilities of language, his "profound conviction that the artist is quasi-divine."[37] Joyce's remark to Budgen, "'Some people who read my book, *A Portrait of the Artist* forget that it is called *A Portrait of the Artist as a Young Man*,'"[38] does not, as Maurice Beebe reminds us, "eradicate the word 'artist.'"[39]

The thesis being advanced in these pages needs qualification. It is based on the belief that nothing in Joyce's work is irrelevant. There must be a reason why Stephen's spiritual development is as it is—in the *Portrait* and the opening of *Ulysses*, the only sections of Joyce's works being studied here. (Whatever happens to Stephen later belongs to another study.) Since the orthodox spiritual life is reversed and inverted, since Stephen suffers from the cause of a blighted spiritual life, and, what is most important, since he does not create art after the composition of the juvenile villanelle, the conclusion must be that his spiritual development is all wrong.

This does not mean that to be right his spiritual development should be the opposite of what occurs in the novel, that he should embrace the Church, Dublin, nationalism, and the university's student body—that he should become a signer of the peace petition, a conforming student who defends the greatness of Tennyson, a seminary student, and, eventually, a Jesuit. Certainly in the world of the novel, the Church and the university are much worse than Stephen. Although his spiritual development is wrong, at least it is a development. They are simply spiritless. But we make a mistake if we blame them for his pride. Dante, who is not especially fond of the existing priesthood, is one of the Western world's great artists, and his spiritual development is orthodox. And, as we shall see later, Hart Crane, starting with a dead Christianity, constructs his major opus on the normal progression of the fivefold division of the spiritual life. To conclude that the *Portrait* is the wrong spiritual development of the artist as a young man does not involve, so far as I can determine, mutually contradictory material.[40]

I do not mean to imply in what follows that if the *Portrait* is not another work, it must therefore be what I claim it is, but contrasting it with two other novels is instructive. The *Portrait* is not *The Man Who Died*. In the Lawrence novel there is an intentional reworking of the Christian mystery: the man awakens to a repudiation of the Passion, to an affirmation of that unique body-soul mystique we associate with Lawrence. There is no question about where the author stands in relation to his protagonist. Neither is the *Portrait* a *Miss Lonelyhearts*. In the West novel it is not so much the characters who are deficient as it is the concept of charity. When Miss Lonelyhearts, who sees himself as a Christ-like figure, rushes to embrace Doyle, he is killed. Love, pity, compassion, charity do not save man; in the protagonist's feverish world the Christ on the wall turns into a bright fly. Nor is Joyce a Robinson Jeffers, whose California in *Roan Stallion* suffers some kind of unnatural awakening and purgation so that she can break away from the mold of humanity. Let us look at Stephen's purgative stage. The scene is comic but not because either Joyce or Stephen is parodying purgation. Stephen does not set out to invert purification; he really believes he is mortifying himself. It is the author's inversion and use of St. John of the Cross that collapse Stephen's self-conscious spiritual exaltation. Joyce is making fun of Stephen at the cash register, not the process of purgation. The latter is at fault because his pride prevents him from seeing that, rather than eliminating his sins, he is in fact committing all seven. Charity is not inoperative; Stephen's pride prevents him from getting outside of himself to love others.

It seems to me that if we accept the kind of close reading that critics give to Joyce's works, then we must extend that analysis to all scenes, which is why I return to a scene toward the beginning of the novel. The first time that Stephen thinks about God, "it made him feel his head very big. He turned over the flyleaf and looked wearily. . . ." The two maladies that cripple spiritual growth, pride and *acedia,* are present in Stephen before Joyce begins to reverse and invert his spiritual life. The rejection of Dante and stage five by the Dedalus family occurs later; by Stephen, at the end of the novel. Further, there is the scene in Chapter II in which

Stephen is accused of heresy. Seen in the light of the dark night stage that traditionally precedes the unitive stage, this scene reveals Stephen as progressing in his reversed, inverted spiritual life. Stephen's pride is not the result of being rejected by a world he never created; on the contrary, commentators on the spiritual life insist that pride is the spiritual malady that prevents growth. Here, again, I concur with Tindall:

> Though determined, like irony and point of view, by the character of Stephen, which is complex enough, the moral idea of A *Portrait* is simple. Joyce condemns pride, the greatest of the seven sins, and commends charity, the greatest of the three virtues. The trouble with Stephen is pride, the greatest of sins. Pride is a defect of charity or love.[41]

It is not coincidental that Stephen is sadly deficient in charity, a virtue which is acquired as one grows spiritually. Here, too, his spiritual progress is reversed and inverted. In Chapter II he enjoys delivering milk and catching glimpses of servants (65-66), but by Chapter V he is blind to the humanity of the flower girl (187) and Rosie (249). To him the Irish are "a race of clodhoppers!" (254) Nowhere in the ending of the novel is there that sustained sense of charity that distinguishes poems of Hopkins such as "Felix Randal." Nor is it coincidental that after his break with the one genuine tie he has with the spiritual life, the Blessed Virgin (165), he breaks with his mother (169), rejects the flower girl and Rosie, and loses Emma (249). Can we afford to overlook the inescapable allusion to Dante in the flower girl and Rosie? We cannot ignore the irony of Stephen's purgative stage any more than we can ignore the irony in the scene of creativity, where he turns toward the wall (226), and the irony in passages such as the one in which the voice calling from beyond the world turns out to be,

"—Hello, Stephanos! —Here comes The Dedalus!" (172)
Stephen is soaring too high.

What prevents him from composing more than a juvenile villanelle, what explains his alienation in both the *Portrait* and *Ulysses*, is his pride, a pride so severe that it cuts him off from the very lifeblood of the mature artist. For the artist as a young man to become the artist as a man, he must learn humility and charity. He must learn in his "own life and away from home and friends what the heart is and what it feels" (257).

IV

T. S. Eliot

ONE FRUITFUL WAY OF APPROACHING ELIOT'S POETRY IS TO compare and contrast his stages with those of Hopkins' poetry. We will begin with the *Ariel Poems* because they "concentrate the notion of rebirth in variations on the theme of Christ's birth." [1] *The Waste Land* is set against the background of awakening and purgation, but "April is the cruellest month" and Stetson is warned to "keep the Dog far hence, that's friend to men, / Or with his nails he'll dig it up again!" Phlebas' death points the way to rebirth, but in Part V the speaker is still sitting upon the shore and the ending is a formal one only.

Hopkins' "New Readings" and "He hath abolished the old drouth" employ the age-old symbolism of sterility and fecundity, one of the ever-present contrasts in Eliot's poetry, in "Journey of the Magi," where the fertility of the "temperate valley" is contrasted with the "very dead of winter." Poem 14 in the Hopkins canon uses in its opening lines the symbolism that begins Eliot's "A Song for Simeon." Pilate, in the fragment, "Pilate," has awakened to a new level of spiritual reality, but although awakened, he is incapable throughout most of the poem of growing spiritually. The description of his spiritual predicament—"dead-alive"—is applicable to the personae in the first three *Ariel Poems*. Spiritual ennui is found in a few early Hopkins' poems. The speaker of "The Beginning of the End" admits, "But now I am so tired I soon shall send / Barely a sigh to thought of hopes forgone." Alienation from the human community, the result of being arrested at the awakening stage, is the keynote of "The Alchemist in the City"; and the speaker of "Myself unholy, from myself unholy" experiences, not the suffering of purgation which leads to illumination, but melancholy. What Pilate, the Magus, Simeon, and the simple soul in "Animula" have in common is a spiritual suspension between birth and death, an inability "to fare forward or retreat" ("Animula").

There is a difference, though, and it is the first of four differences between Hopkins' and Eliot's poetry that will be discussed. Pilate has doubts about the meaning of the Redemption, but he has "a hope if so it be, / A hope of an approved device," and he elects the purgative stage: he finally elects real suffering, imitation of the agony of the Passion. The speakers in the *Ariel Poems* have their doubts. The Magus knows "there was a Birth, certainly, / We had evidence and no doubt." Its significance, however, like the symbolism of the second stanza, escapes him, for he asks for the peace of literal death only: "I should be glad of another death." Simeon rejects the purgative way. The matter-of-fact way in which he summarizes his past (stanza 2) betrays the meaninglessness of purgation without suffering. The real test of spiritual growth he rejects (stanzas 3 and 4). "Marina" is a transitional poem between awakening and purgation. On the one hand, it is the one of the *Ariel Poems* most clearly in the awakening stage, since the speaker awakens to the possibility of spiritual growth and a higher vision:

This form, this face, this life
Living to live in a world of time beyond me; let me
Resign my life for this life, my speech for that unspoken,
The awakened, lips parted, the hope, the new ships.

On the other hand, the epigraph, the horror of Hercules' awakening, alludes to awakening inextricably united with purgation, just as the images of sin are "dissolved in place" by the "grace" of the vision of Marina. "Marina" is intimately related to *Ash Wednesday*, itself a fusion of awakening and purgation.

At this point it might be well to remind the reader of the inevitable overlapping of the stages. This reminder is not so important for Joyce as it is for Hopkins and Eliot because Joyce is *using* the stages as a framework against which we are to understand Stephen, nor is it so important for Crane, who is *using*, in a different sense from Joyce, the stages as a framework in which lies contemporary man's salvation. Joyce had the advantage of looking back at the past and evaluating the artist as a young man, and Crane had the advantage of setting out to create, however feebly he discerned the final form of some of the parts, his major poem on the possibility of a spiritual life in the twentieth century. With Hopkins and Eliot we face the problem of attempting to indicate subtle shifts in emphasis in poetry written over a period of a lifetime as the authors were themselves growing.

Another way of approaching this first difference in Eliot's poetry is by contrasting the attitude toward the unitive stage in Hopkins' early poems and that in the *Ariel Poems*. We saw that in Hopkins' early poetry the mistake of the speaker, or, rather, his immaturity in the spiritual life, lies in his desire to rush through the stages and reach the mystical experience as quickly as possible. From "New Readings," an early draft of which appears in July, 1864, to

"Nondum," 1866, and "The Habit of Perfection," an early version of which is dated January, 1866, is a span of only two years and eighteen completed poems. His immature desire accounts for the pseudo-asceticism in poems 9 through 17. Between the time of "Rosa Mystica," the poem that begins the transition from pseudo-mysticism to genuine asceticism, or *The Wreck*, the first great mature poem, to "Thou art indeed just, Lord, if I contend" is a span of fourteen years and forty-six completed poems. And at this point Hopkins is still struggling with the test of total humility and self-abnegation, still praying for divine assistance: "Mine, O thou lord of life, send my roots rain."

Simeon's problem, unlike that of the Magus, who does not know, is that he knows what constitutes spiritual growth, what tests must be mastered in order for the possibility of the final stage to occur, but he refuses to elect purgation: "Not for me the martyrdom, the ecstasy of thought and prayer, / Not for me the ultimate vision." The problem of the "irresolute and selfish" simple soul in "Animula" is that it refuses to accept the "heavy burden of the growing soul."

The Wreck and *Ash Wednesday* stand in a comparable position in relation to the poetry that precedes them, the early poetry and the *Ariel Poems*, in that each marks a transition from a concern with mysticism to asceticism. But whereas *The Wreck* initiates genuine asceticism, the degree of beginners, because this is where spiritual growth must commence, whether or not infused contemplation will occur, *Ash Wednesday* initiates genuine asceticism, the degree of beginners, because this is the way to achieve infused contemplation. Further, whereas the poems following *The Wreck* exhibit a progression within the spiritual life, the problem facing Simeon, the acceptance of the requisites for the possibility of achieving the unitive stage, becomes by the time of Chorus X from "The Rock" to Part V of "The Dry Salvages" to *The Cocktail Party* a secondary consideration, replaced by the more important one, the discovery of the spiritual life, the awakening to the meaning of the birth witnessed by the Magus. If the poems of this period "may be called the *Purgatorio* period," [2] it is or is not an elected purgation, depending on the persona. That Eliot understood the importance of awakening to the acceptance of pain and suffering at the time he was writing the *Ariel Poems* and *Ash Wednesday* is clear from his essay on Dante [3] and Parts II, I, and III of *Ash Wednesday* (1930), which were published separately in 1927, 1928, and 1929, the dates for the first three *Ariel Poems*.

We can turn to *Ash Wednesday*, the poem which places a greater emphasis on active purgation than do the *Ariel Poems*, and to the role of the female in their poetry, the second difference. In the fragment, "A Voice from the World," the "remember'd sweetness" of a loved one, who has entered the convent, torments the speaker, preventing him from overcoming his sensual desires:

> How shall I search, who never sought?
> How turn my passion-pastured thought
> To gentle manna and simple bread?

He requests that she lead him to purgation and, therefore, to a greater spiritual reality, in the passage, quoted in the chapter on Hopkins, beginning, "Teach me the paces that you went." In *Ash Wednesday* the speaker must overcome the torture of the "rose of memory / Rose of forgetfulness," the "torment / Of love unsatisfied / The greater torment / Of love satisfied." It is the Lady who leads him to genuine purgation. In Part I he prays for divine assistance. In Part II he elects suffering. That is, his symbolic death, the death of the "old man," occurs in Part II, the first of the sections to be published separately.

Both "Rosa Mystica" and *Ash Wednesday* employ the

Dantean symbolism of the garden and the rose. In the earlier poem the rose is first Mary, then Christ. In the later poem "the single Rose / Is now the Garden / Where all loves end." The rose and garden lead to Mary in Part II, through "the word only" that concludes Part III and "the token of the word unheard, unspoken" in Part IV, and then directly to Christ in Part V. Mary "plays in grace her part / About man's beating heart" in poem 60; *Ash Wednesday* concludes with a prayer to "blessèd sister, holy mother, spirit of the fountain, spirit of the garden" to intercede for the speaker.

Eliot's handling of the female points up the second difference, the difference in purgation between his and Hopkins' poetry. In Hopkins' poetry the lady of "A Voice" never becomes symbolic of the Blessed Virgin in any kind of way the reader can realize. In "A Voice" and "Marina" the females are compared to stars—and as Stephen in the *Portrait* knows, the morning star is Mary's emblem—but they never become realized females; at most they are symbolic of hope. And the similarity ends here, for Hopkins' poetry lacks the felt reality of the female. The speaker in "A Voice" merely declaims, "My tears are but a cloud of rain; / My passion like a foolish wind / Lifts them a little way above." It is impossible for the reader to feel the reality of the female in this poem or the one whose earthly love is being rejected in "The Beginning of the End."

Hopkins' females are not figures of Mary as they are in the *Portrait,* where a rejection of the Blessed Virgin *means* a loss of his mother, the flower girl, Rosie, and Emma; his females are not the Virgin in the process of transmutation as she is in *The Bridge.* Nowhere in Hopkins' poetry is there the felt reality of the female as distraction, as temptation as in Part III of *Ash Wednesday.* Hopkins' poetry lacks the Mary figures of Beatrice and Matilda as in Part IV of this poem.

This is another way of stating that although Hopkins

and Eliot recognize the essence of purgation, the pain and suffering that make possible "our peace in His will" (Part VI of *Ash Wednesday*), the desires of the self which must be overcome in Hopkins' poetry are not what they are in *Ash Wednesday*. (In *The Bridge* purgation will overcome a third type of self-orientation.)

Eliot's comments, "We are not concerned with the authors' *beliefs*, but with orthodoxy of sensibility and with the sense of tradition, our degree of approaching 'that region where dwell the vast hosts of the dead.'... And the most ethically orthodox of the more eminent writers of my time is Mr. Joyce," [4] take on an added meaning when we put their work side by side. By ironically utilizing Dantean imagery and symbolism, Joyce turns Stephen's initiation to the spiritual life inside out, for the wading girl and Emma, an inverted Beatrice, awaken him to the life of the body and the life of the artist. For Eliot, "the *Vita Nuova* has a special importance. ..." It is not, he continues, "meant as a description of what he *consciously* felt on his meeting with Beatrice, but rather as a description of what that meant on mature reflection upon it." [5] The Lady of *Ash Wednesday*, who "can stand at once as Beatrice or a saint or the Virgin herself, as well as being an idealized beautiful woman," [6] awakens the speaker to a "new life." It is she who purifies his love from earthly to spiritual, who can "redeem / The time. Redeem / The unread vision in the higher dream" (Part IV).

There are other parallels between the *Portrait* and *Ash Wednesday*. Chapter III of the novel can be read as an inverted *Ash Wednesday*. At the opening of this chapter, Stephen imagines his soul taking the form of a peacock (106). Because of his pride he cannot atone for his sins, "the fountains of sanctifying grace having ceased to refresh his soul" (107). In Part I of the poem the speaker, who sees himself as an agèd eagle, "cannot drink / There, where trees flower, and springs flow, for there is nothing again."

Stephen's one genuine link with the spiritual life is the Blessed Virgin, and Chapter III is punctuated by prayers to her; *Ash Wednesday* is partially built upon the repetition of liturgical cadences. At the beginning of the retreat, "Stephen's heart had withered up like a flower of the desert that feels the simoom coming from afar" (112); one of the basic contrasts of Eliot's poem is the garden-rose-desert symbolism. Early in the retreat Stephen is expected to experience the symbolic death of the natural man (115), which death occurs in Part II of the poem.

One evening during the retreat, as Stephen walks home, the laughter of a girl strikes his heart. More than a distraction, she, like "the broadbacked figure drest in blue and green" in Part III, brings temptation and a sense of shame and guilt (119). Following the retreat Stephen ascends the stairs to his room, "through a region of viscid gloom." In the field below, hideous creatures make manifest his sins to him (139-141). The first two stanzas of Part III are also an ascent, carrying the speaker above the twisting shapes on the stairs below. On the way to confession Stephen "walked on and on through illlit streets, fearing to stand still for a moment lest it might seem that he held back from what awaited him, fearing to arrive at that towards which he still turned with longing" (144), a major movement of *Ash Wednesday*. And, finally, Stephen's receiving of Communion is prefaced by a dream (149), the time of the opening of Part VI of the poem.

The difference between Joyce and Eliot is that where the former is ironic, particularly in Stephen's illumination following confession and in his purgative stage, the latter is not. Where he and Hopkins differ is in the ascent of Part III, for here, as elsewhere in the poem, it is the desires of the flesh that must be refined in the purgatorial fire. The Beatrice figure in *Ash Wednesday* is a female who awakens the speaker to a "new life" and who, as a female, contains both the distraction of "the broadbacked figure drest in blue and green" and the intercession of "the veiled sister." At the same time that the speaker's earthly love is being purified, he is awakening to the possibility of a transformed earthly life and the possibility of spiritual growth and a higher spiritual vision. In this sense, "Marina," published after *Ash Wednesday*, is an advance upon that poem because the purgation of the deadly sins is behind Pericles, and ahead of him lies hope in the future.

There is another parallel in these works by Hopkins, Joyce, and Eliot (and Crane as well). Embarked on the way of purgation and imitation of Christ, the speaker of Hopkins' poems receives strength and divine assistance to continue spiritual growth, and he experiences the spiritual world crashing through the natural world. The same theme is treated, ironically, in the *Portrait*. After Stephen meets his sins face to face, he rushes to the window, vomiting. Lifting the sash, he gazes upon a radiant world, "and amid peace and shimmering lights and quiet fragrance he made a covenant with his heart" (142). On the way to confession he reflects on the transformed girls (144). In Part VI of *Ash Wednesday* the speaker, at the window, experiences a rejuvenation of heart, mind, will, and senses.[7]

That the poem is inconclusive, that the speaker is caught in "the time of tension between dying and birth" (Part VI), does not weaken the poem. On the contrary, in terms of the spiritual life, the strength of *Ash Wednesday* is its inconclusiveness, its fidelity to spiritual growth. One does not pass through the purgative stage to have it terminate at a given moment, never to reappear. One does not cleanse himself spiritually, never again to sin or to be tempted. In the third group of Hopkins' mature poems, the speaker is still wrestling with the critical test of spiritual growth. One of the ironies of Stephen's purgation is his humiliation and shame because he will never be completely free from sin (156).

Within *Ash Wednesday* the speaker does grow spiritually; he does overcome the despair and frustration of Part I; he is able in Part VI to perceive a transformed world of nature; he is able to hope for divine assistance and further growth.

Before we continue with Eliot's works, we must return to the problem of the separation of ascetical and mystical theology. In the introduction to this study, I attempted to indicate how authorities disagree, one group insisting on the separation and another insisting that the spiritual life is best studied under one heading. To eliminate considerations which would defeat the purpose of this study, to determine if there is a ground common to the four, I elected to follow commentators such as Goodier, de Guibert, and Garrigou-Lagrange, who do not adhere to the separation.

This problem is relevant to St. John of the Cross and, therefore, to Eliot because there are numerous allusions to the Saint's writings in his poetry. In Book I, Chapter I, of the *Ascent of Mount Carmel*, he outlines the structure of his two most important prose expositions: Book I of the *Ascent* is devoted to the active purgation of the senses; Book II, to the active purgation of the spirit (understanding); Book III, to the active purgation of the spirit (memory and will). The fourth part is the *Dark Night*, Book I of which is devoted to the passive purgation of the senses; Book II, to the passive purgation of the spirit.

A problem in the interpretation of St. John of the Cross' mystical theology is whether or not his beginners' and proficients' degrees conform to the traditional threefold division. Fr. Parente, who insists on the separation, is of the opinion that they do not.[8] I prefer to follow Fr. Garrigou-Lagrange, who does not adhere to the separation.[9] It follows that for him St. John of the Cross' degrees conform to the traditional threefold division, that his beginners' stage is the first stage and his proficients' stage is the second stage. Both Fr. Garrigou-Lagrange and Fr. Poulain, who insists on the

separation,[10] judge that for the Carmelite mystic passive
purification is the distinguishing characteristic that indicates
the exercitant is being led from the meditation of the beginners' degree to the contemplation of the proficients' degree.
Yet this "second conversion of passive purification of the
senses in order to enter the illuminative way of proficients," [11]
cannot be applied conclusively to the stages in Eliot's poetry.
His poetry always returns to the awakening and purgative
stages.

Following Strothmann and Ryan, Unger, and Smith, we
can look at the poetry of this period in the light of St. John
of the Cross.[12] *Ash Wednesday* is the beginning stage, the
active privation of all pleasures and the mortification of all
desires. In each of the six sections there is an active purgation—whether it be a prayer for assistance, a mortification of
the sensual desires, an election of the purgatorial fire—which
allows the poem to move forward. "Sovegna vos," which
alludes to Arnaut Daniel's election of the purgatorial fire in
the *Purgatorio,* XXVI.145-148, and the temptation of the
female during the ascent of the stairway define the sensual
nature as that which the speaker is purging. In view of the
utilization, rather than the voiding, or the refining, of the
memory, *Ash Wednesday* cannot be a stage beyond active
purgation of sense,

> for until the desires are lulled to sleep through the mortifica-
> tion of the sensual nature, and until at last the sensual nature
> itself is at rest from them, so that they make not war upon
> the spirit, the soul goes not forth to true liberty and to the
> fruition of union with its Beloved (*Ascent* I.xv).

Although passages in the poem may allude to material in
Book II of the *Ascent,* the active purgation of the spirit,[13]
these passages are still within the beginning stage, for the
distinguishing characteristic is that God leads the beginner

into the illuminative way, the degree of proficients (*Dark Night* I.i). Nowhere in *Ash Wednesday* is there any proof that the speaker is receiving divine touches, that God is leading him into a higher spiritual state. Even taking into account the difference in the female, *Ash Wednesday* is close in spirit to the first group of Hopkins' mature poems, for both are concerned with admission of sin, recognition that the spiritual life is the true life, admission that spiritual growth is impossible without divine assistance, and active prayer, penance, detachment, and mortification. In summary, *The Hollow Men* (accepting the findings of Strothmann and Ryan) is an awakening to the spiritual life, the first three *Ariel Poems* are awakenings without growth, and *Ash Wednesday* and "Marina" are awakenings with purgations.

After examining active purgation of the senses, the Carmelite mystic turns to active purgation of the spirit: the understanding through faith, the memory through hope, and the will through charity. As early as Book II, Chapter XIII, of the *Ascent*, the author analyzes the signs whereby the person may lay aside the task of discursive meditation. It is increasingly evident from the final third of Book II on that he is describing God's assisting the soul by divine touches.

Between *Ash Wednesday* and the *Four Quartets,* Eliot moves to active purgation of the spirit. Thomas in *Murder in the Cathedral* and Harry in *The Family Reunion* are more advanced in the spiritual life than the speaker in *Ash Wednesday* in that neither must purge his sensual nature. Instead, Thomas must purge his will through charity, and Harry, his memory through hope. Celia in *The Cocktail Party* also will make greater spiritual progress than the speaker of the penitential poem. And all three, unlike the personae of the earlier poems, imitate, with qualifications to be examined later, Christ's "great sacrifice" by electing to sacrifice themselves. There is no indisputable proof, however, that any one of them experiences divine touches leading him into the illuminative stage. At best we can say that they are not "most of us" but are possibly destined for sainthood.

Let us look at this problem from another direction. Joyce is eliminated because there is nothing in Hopkins' and Eliot's poetry to compare with the cessation of Stephen's faculties and the penetration of the dark presence in Chapter II of the *Portrait,* and his spiritual progress results in isolation from God and man. Since Hopkins does not seem to be indebted to the Carmelite mystic as Eliot definitely is, I discussed his poetry according to the treatment of the stages by Fr. de Guibert and others. But certainly his poetry exhibits orthodox spiritual growth, and certainly divine assistance is absolutely essential regardless of the stage in which we place any one of his poems. Grace is operative from *The Wreck* to the last line of the completed poems. Both Hopkins and Eliot recognize that spiritual growth is a combination of active purgation, imitation of Christ, and God's grace. In *Ash Wednesday* "God said / Shall these bones live? shall these / Bones live?" (Part II) The speaker receives "strength beyond hope and despair / Climbing the third stair" (Part III). Throughout, he resigns himself to divine assistance.

Of the two, though, Hopkins emphasizes the operation of grace more, and the reason is that whereas he is primarily interested in what is involved in spiritual growth, Eliot is primarily interested in reaffirming the means for discovering the spiritual life, for discovering grace. Grace is given a special prominence in "Little Gidding" because while actively praying, hoping, and converting lust into love, modern man, unaware of grace, awakens to God's assisting him to acquire faith, hope, and charity—awakens to God's grace. Hopkins stresses spiritual growing; Eliot, spiritual awakening. Eliot has never written any "terrible" sonnets.

To conclude, for the moment, this short discussion of

Eliot's use of St. John of the Cross, we see there are two types of allusion: one which helps to designate what is taking place, active purgation (*Ash Wednesday*), and one which points ahead to the possibility of passive purgation (Part III of "East Coker"). Nowhere is there any conclusive proof that passive purgation is taking place or has taken place. Of the characters who, at first glance, may qualify as exercitants beyond the beginning stage of active purgation, Thomas has one passage that is too ambiguous to be decisive, Harry's awakening is partial only, and Celia's growth occurs off stage. Sister Mary Gerard's conclusion deserves quoting. Studying the *Four Quartets,* especially "Burnt Norton," in reference to the wheel image, the search for the pattern, the description of the two ways of achieving the mystical union, the cyclical theory of time, and redemption through liberation, she decides that "it is certain that the definitive association of the *Four Quartets* with St. John of the Cross represents an oversimplification, if not a misdirected emphasis." [14]

Parallels can be drawn between *Murder in the Cathedral* and *The Wreck.* Each has its source in the death of a real person; central to each is the problem of acting and suffering; each is primarily concerned with the effect on the audience—in *The Wreck,* the speaker; in *Murder,* the chorus. In the process of interpreting the nun's death, the speaker tries to determine why she acted as she did; why she suffered death; whether or not her death was willed by her, an act of suicide, or joyful acceptance of the agony of the divine pattern presented to her to elect or to reject. We can trace his awakening through his questions in stanza 25 to his answer in stanza 27: "No, but it was not these." Her acceptance of the divine will is her imitation of Christ, her participation in the Passion and Redemption (stanza 28), and her rebirth through the Incarnation (stanzas 29 and 30). To the question, "Is the shipwreck then a harvest, does tempest carry the grain for thee?" (stanza 31) the speaker comes to learn that the way to salvation, his and mankind's, is the way of the nun: "Now burn, new born to the world. . . . Let him easter in us."

Murder suffers by comparison, an unfair one because of the medium in which Eliot is working, since Thomas tells the audience about the problem of acting and suffering. We follow his realization through his articulation of the problem, in his first speech in Part I, and of the resolution, in his concluding speech in Part I. His lengthy exposition in the Interlude and statements such as "I have therefore only to make perfect my will" weaken our felt realization of his spiritual suffering. Where the speaker in *The Wreck* discovers that "she that weather sees one thing, one; / Has one fetch in her: she rears herself to divine / Ears," Thomas tells us in Part II that

> I have had a tremor of bliss, a wink of heaven, a whisper,
> And I would no longer be denied; all things
> Proceed to a joyful consummation.

This passage may indicate that Thomas has had a divine touch leading him into the illuminative stage, but in view of the lack of any intense suffering on his part, it is difficult to argue that he has experienced passive purgation. Eliot is intentionally ambiguous here. Undoubtedly God is assisting Thomas to reach his decision, but it is more consistent with the meaning of the drama, that man must elect to bend his will to God's will, and more consistent with the corpus of Eliot's works to read this passage as Thomas' discovery of the higher reality of the timeless that impinges on time. And even if it is a divine touch, it presents no problem. Thomas is not one "of us"; he is, after all, Saint Thomas à Becket.

The power of *Murder* is in the ritual drama. The theater audience is drawn into the chorus and awakens as the women awaken. Spiritually apathetic at first, the chorus comes to understand the meaning of Thomas' martyrdom, and the drama ends with praise of God, reconciliation to the divine pattern, and acceptance of the Incarnation, Passion, and Redemption. The importance of *Murder* for this study is that it brings its author closer to the central consideration of Hopkins—the movement from submission to, acceptance of, and abandonment in God's will and the pain and joy that are involved in that movement—and of Joyce—Stephen's refusal to break his pride with the resulting alienation from God and the human community. We can sketch in this movement in Eliot's works from the speaker's prayer in Part VI of *Ash Wednesday* that "our peace [is] in His will," through the Choruses from "The Rock," with the phrases in Choruses I and VIII, "Make perfect your will" and "Let us therefore make perfect our will," to Thomas' realization in *Murder*: "A martyrdom is never the design of man; for the true martyr is he who has become the instrument of God, who has lost his will in the will of God, not lost it but found it, for he has found freedom in submission to God." Those passages in the Choruses which deal with the active acquisition of faith, hope, and, most of all, charity lead into *The Family Reunion*. A passage in Chorus V, when coupled with Mrs. Dedalus' parting words to her son, can be read as a commentary on his type of spiritual predicament: "If humility and purity be not in the heart, they are not in the home: and if they are not in the home, they are not in the City."

In its statement of intention an excerpt of a letter from Eliot to Martin Browne tells how certain elements were to be fused in *The Family Reunion*.[15] Prior to the interview between Harry and Mary, Agatha perceptively comments to Mary that "there is no decision to be made; / The decision will be made by powers beyond us / Which now and then emerge" (I.ii). A few minutes later Harry says to Mary, "I was part of the design / As well as you. But what was the design?" (I.ii) As a result of not understanding his relationship to the divine pattern, he has lost hope (I.ii). The attraction of Mary is meant to be "a possible 'way of escape,' and the Furies (for the Furies are *divine* instruments, not simple hell-hounds) come in the nick of time to warn him away from this evasion—though at that moment he misunderstands their function." [16] In order for this scene to make sense, Harry should reject the divine pattern, the "design," the "powers beyond us"—represented by the Furies—by accepting the " 'way of escape' " offered by Mary. That is, his rejection of the "design" means his acceptance of Mary's love as an excuse for not sacrificing himself, or his acceptance of the "design" means sacrificing the " 'way of escape' " offered by Mary. In the play Harry neither accepts Mary's love, nor rejects it for spiritual growth, so that when he rejects the Furies (I.ii), he has neither Mary's love nor hope (I.ii), and "the past" is still "unredeemable" (I.iii).

When in the second scene mentioned in the letter, Harry rejects Agatha's love, it is a sacrifice because Agatha has become a mother to him (II.ii). When the "design" is presented this time, Harry sacrifices the possibility of happiness offered by Agatha and accepts the divine pattern (II.ii). In order for his action to be a sacrifice, it must involve suffering. His destination lies "somewhere on the other side of despair. / To the worship in the desert, the thirst and deprivation. . . ." (II.ii) In this respect Agatha's stepping "into the place which the Eumenides had occupied" (II.ii) is her election of the "design" and her sacrifice, for she tells Harry, who has become a son to her, "You must go" (II.ii).

In terms of Harry's spiritual growth, the play fails in the area of charity because his decision to accept the "design" should be motivated by love, yet he does not know why he sacrifices, why he has "this election" (II.ii). His explanation, "My advice has come from quite a different quarter" (II.ii), is ambiguous. If Eliot means a divine touch leading him into the illuminative stage, rather than an awakening to the need for purgation, it is at odds with his inability to love. He is a spiritual snob with his aunts and uncles, he fails to grow in love toward his mother, he does not experience remorse over the death of his wife, and his exit kills his mother. Years later Eliot went so far as to call him "an insufferable prig." [17]

Now we can understand the ambiguity of the scene with Mary (I.ii). In rejecting the Furies, Harry does not accept Mary, not because he recognizes that acceptance of her love will remove the possibility of sacrifice, but because he is incapable of love. In fact, his spiritual malady comes close to pride, in having the Furies pursue him: "They are much too clever / To admit you into our world" (I.ii). If his sacrifice were motivated by love of God and, therefore, love of God's creatures, then it would be more meaningful because recognizing that the way of suffering is more important than the possibility of happiness that human love offers, Harry would be rejecting a very real human attraction. This is why in his exit he elicits little sympathy from us. In the light of "Little Gidding," he fails to discover grace because he fails to work at acquiring the three virtues. Consequently, his awakening is only partial: "I know that I have made a decision / In a moment of clarity, and now I feel dull again" (II.ii).

Unfortunately, The Family Reunion contains this flaw because the intention was to extend the drama of Thomas to a wider social sphere. Harry's expiation of the family curse is supposed to effect a family reunion. When Agatha says to him, "It is possible / You are the consciousness of your unhappy family, / Its bird sent flying through the purgatorial flame" (II.ii), we can see in him a corrective to the type of flight proposed by Stephen, whose consciousness is turned inward and whose flight is into the nightmare of history. But since Eliot never wrote the sequels suggested in the letter, we have to look at other works to find charity in operation.

The Four Quartets synthesizes the elements of Eliot's

previous work. "East Coker" is close in spirit to St. John of the Cross. The lines, "I said to my soul, be still, and let the dark come upon you / Which shall be the darkness of God" (Part III), are in the beginners' degree; they point ahead to the possibility of divine touches which will lead the soul into the proficients' degree. The passage in Part III beginning, "I said to my soul, be still, and wait without hope / For hope would be hope for the wrong thing," alludes to active purgation of spirit and points ahead to the possibility of infused contemplation. The passage in Part III beginning, "You say I am repeating / Something I have said before," alludes to the summation of active purgation of the senses in Book I, Chapter XIII, of the *Ascent,* which includes the famous passage beginning, "In order to arrive at having pleasure in everything, / Desire to have pleasure in nothing." Part IV of "East Coker" is active purgation with divine assistance. It involves a recognition of such assistance; an admission of sin, man's fallen condition; an election of the pain and suffering of purgation; and a recognition that the spiritual life, especially imitation of Christ, is man's salvation: "The dripping blood our only drink, / The bloody flesh our only food." The ending of "East Coker,"

> We must be still and still moving
> Into another intensity
> For a further union, a deeper communion,

seems to point toward an advance upon the beginning stage, but "Figlia del tuo figlio, / Queen of Heaven" in Part IV of "The Dry Salvages" returns us to *Ash Wednesday,* and Part V of "The Dry Salvages" marks a resolution in spiritual growth. Those who can "apprehend / The point of intersection of the timeless / With time" are saints; "most of us" have "only the unattended / Moment" and must practice "prayer, observance, discipline, thought and action."

This resolution constitutes a third difference between the poetry of Hopkins and Eliot. After Hopkins' early poems there is little mention of a final mystical union. Instead, his poetry exhibits a gradual movement from admission of sin to the terrible struggle to achieve complete humility and self-abnegation. Eliot's poetry, on the other hand, presents a curious cyclical pattern. Simeon has an inkling of where spiritual growth may lead, but he refuses to accept what must precede union or even illumination. *Ash Wednesday* is the inevitable first step, active purgation of the senses. Chorux X from "The Rock" contains a resolution comparable to that in "The Dry Salvages." Since union is too difficult for most men—"ecstasy is too much pain"—they should be thankful for what light they have, "the little lights for which our bodily vision is made." Then *Murder in the Cathedral* and *The Family Reunion* attempt to extend spiritual growth to active purgation of the spirit. Both, however, are weak in terms of this progression, the first because Thomas' struggle is reported to us, the second because Harry's lack of understanding and charity defeats the intended meaning of the sacrifice. When we get to "East Coker," we are back to *Ash Wednesday*: admission of sin, and so on, and Part V of "The Dry Salvages" is another resolution, which separates those destined for sainthood from "most of us." Part V of "The Dry Salvages," like *Ash Wednesday*, parallels the end of Hopkins' early period, the turning from passivity to activity.

"Little Gidding" begins again the cycle started by the penitential poem and shows how the five modes of asceticism in Part V of "The Dry Salvages" can be practiced. Part I is concerned with prayer and the observance of Little Gidding's devotional community; Part II, with the acceptance of the discipline of the purgatorial fire; Part III, with the use of memory (thought), with detachment "from self and from things and from persons," and with purification "of the motive / In the ground of our beseeching"; Part IV, with divine assistance and election of the purgatorial fire (action); and Part V, with another resolution that points toward salvation: the union of the fire and the rose. The refining fire which transforms lust to love in Parts II, IV, and V is the refining fire of Arnaut Daniel in the *Purgatorio,* which brings us back to "Sovegna vos" in *Ash Wednesday.*

I do not mean to imply that the spiritual life in Eliot's poetry is deficient because it never successfully leaves the beginning stage of active purgation (in the division of St. John of the Cross, which Eliot, unlike Hopkins, uses as a guide). Purgation is always present in Hopkins' poetry, too. And in the *Four Quartets* there is more emphasis on imitation of Christ and acquisition of the virtues than there is in *Ash Wednesday.* But the pattern in Eliot's poetry is different from that in Hopkins' poetry, and I think it is best understood in relation to Eliot's conception of time and the Incarnation, the fourth and final difference in their poetry.

Had Hopkins never written a line beyond the three stanzas in *The Wreck* beginning, "Not out of his bliss / Springs the stress felt," we would have in these stanzas all we need to know about the significance of the Incarnation, and Its extension, the Redemption and the Mystical Body. From *The Wreck* on the Incarnation is a fact; it is there in the imagery, the structure, the meaning of each poem. There are no long passages trying to narrow the circle about the Word so that it is finally made lucid; it is the fact from which all of his poems spring. It is as if Eliot devoted a lifetime, through *Ash Wednesday,* the *Coriolan* fragments, the Choruses from "The Rock," to the *Four Quartets,* to arrive at the Jesuit's metaphor, "it rides time like riding a river." This treatment is partially explained by his method of encircling, expanding, contracting around and about—drawing the audience from the wheel to the still point—so that in the process the audience comes to perceive the real meaning of the Word. It is partially explained by his attempt to synthesize disparates such as Christianity, Heraclitus, the *Bhagavad-Gita*, Hinduism, Buddhism so that the audience can see what is fundamental to all. It is partially explained by his view of the human condition.

For Hopkins history is the working out of Christ's "great sacrifice," through love, in pain and agony, which redeemed and redeems time. The Incarnation is the fundamental reality for any and all time: "it rides time like riding a river." Man's salvation consists in his imitating, on a human level, Christ's "great sacrifice" and with God's grace, which perfects nature, becoming a member of Christ's Mystical Body. For Eliot modern man's history is a cycle of empty, frustrating, meaningless experiences. Since he is so self-centered and so given to sensual pleasures that he cannot love, he finds himself revolving on the wheel of defeating experiences. Although the Incarnation redeemed and redeems time (Part V of "The Dry Salvages"), he has only in rare moments the "hint half guessed, the gift half understood." Eliot is drawing the audience, who has lost not merely the humility to admit sin but even the belief in sin, into the discovery that the way to break out of the sterility of contemporary life's endless cycle of drugs is the spiritual life. What I am claiming is that Eliot is not really interested in spiritual growth that leads to illumination and on to union so much as he is interested in affirming the necessity of the spiritual life.[18]

Before we continue with Eliot's treatment of time, we can summarize the features in his poetry that distinguish it from Hopkins' poetry. Together they form a unified view of the spiritual life in the contemporary world. First, the personae in the *Ariel Poems* are in a spiritual predicament because they reject active purgation. Two, since lust is the great sin of the modern world, the strong felt reality of the female and the desires of the flesh are converted in the purgatorial fire, which must be elected, to the Beatrice and the Virgin figures and to love. Three, the pattern of the spiritual life is cyclical, always returning to the beginning stage. Four, the view of history is cyclical. The Incarnation redeemed and redeems time, but the Word has been lost in the modern world.

A motif that runs throughout Eliot's works is that of the once beautiful experience, misunderstood at the time and now lost, except for a trace retained in the memory and tormenting in the knowledge that it can never be recaptured in its original form. If the speaker can somehow return to it, by seeing it outside of the intervening time that has altered it, he can understand its significance and the cycle of history subsequent to it. Approaching it "restores the experience / In a different form" (Part II of "The Dry Salvages"). What he does is to use the memory (Part III of "Little Gidding"). This utilization of the memory as a means to the redemption of the personal past almost precludes, so long as it is being utilized, the possibility of spiritual growth beyond active purgation. On the one hand, active purgation of the spirit, according to St. John of the Cross, voids, or refines, the memory through hope. On the other hand, infused contemplation causes a cessation of the faculties of memory, imagination, and will. Spiritual growth is outside the considerations of Eliot's poetry, which are: how to redeem the personal past, how to break the meaningless cycle of history, how to establish the validity of the spiritual life. Spiritual growth is possible only for someone like Celia in *The Cocktail Party*, the redemption of whose personal past has already been achieved.

Eliot's use of memory is a fusion of a typical Henry James fictional situation and St. John of the Cross. In one type of Jamesian fiction, a narrator is haunted by the memory of a prior experience, which, because of the narrator's failure, did not come to fruition—usually a relationship that could have developed into love. In the process of attempting to discover what went wrong, the narrator can begin to understand the truth of the experience, and, as in the case of *The Sacred Fount* and *The Turn of the Screw*, begin to see the spiritual potentialities in the experience. I assume this was the intention of the last stanza of Eliot's "Portrait of a Lady," although it is not successful. Perhaps it is better seen in *The Family Reunion*, for Harry is haunted by memories of his childhood. If we add to this St. John of the Cross, for whom a persistent memory of God is a characteristic of the night of the senses, we have a typical Eliot situation. The implication of Part V of "The Dry Salvages" is that the "hints and guesses" are God-given. The timeless reality of the Incarnation, which impinges on the temporal reality of the secular world, stirs the memory to search for Him. These "hints and guesses" coincide with the memory of the unfulfilled experience. At the same time that Harry penetrates to the truth of his childhood and his marriage, he discovers the existence of a spiritual realm.

Of the stages of the spiritual life, the first, active purgation, is the one that can best be utilized for "most of us," those for whom the religious-spiritual concepts are lost. With its characteristics of detachment, mortification, prayer, penance, and humility, this stage appeals to man's sense of responsibility for the salvation of his soul at the same time it emphasizes God's assistance and urges man's recognition that his self-centeredness causes lust. Human love can follow active purgation of lust. Humility is the prerequisite for human understanding and love. How much Eliot is writing from personal experience and how much he is assimilating the discipline which for the majority of people in the contemporary world is the key to understanding self and the self's relation to that which is outside it is speculation, but the spiritual life also accomplishes the "inner freedom from the practical desire. . . ." (Part II of "Burnt Norton")

By detaching himself from the wheel in the search for the lost moment, man can view his past. He can humble himself by admitting to himself that his failure is his inability to get outside of the prison of his self, which produces lust. If he can make this painful admission, he can mortify and purge himself of those sensual and selfish desires which eat away at his soul, which redeems his past and prepares him for a better—that is, spiritual—future and the possibility of love. Hence the persistence of the *Vita Nuova* experience in Eliot's poetry. This unceasing exploration into the meaning of the past (Part V of "Little Gidding") redeems time, for

> If all time is eternally present
> All time is unredeemable.
> What might have been is an abstraction
> Remaining a perpetual possibility
> Only in a world of speculation (Part I of "Burnt Norton").

At the moment the speaker arrives at the lost moment in the rose-garden, the still point in the turning wheel in his own past, which redeems his personal past, he intersects the historic moment which redeemed all time, the Incarnation, the timeless moment in time. This intersection unites him with his human heritage, "our, and Adam's curse" (Part IV of "East Coker"). The knowledge that the Incarnation, Passion, and Redemption are "the sharp compassion of the healer's art" (Part IV of "East Coker"), done through love, assists him to purify his lust into love by imitating Christ's "great sacrifice." "Little Gidding" is important because it shows how if man elects purgation and the redemption of his personal past, he intersects the timeless. By believing, in Part I, he discovers the grace that assists him in acquiring faith: "Here, the intersection of the timeless moment / Is England and nowhere. Never and always." By hoping, in Part IV, he discovers the grace of the "dove descending" that assists him in acquiring hope. By loving, in Parts IV and V, he discovers the grace that assists him in acquiring charity.

The choice is man's: "We only live, only suspire / Consumed by either fire or fire" (Part IV). Returning momentarily to *The Family Reunion,* we see that Harry's failure to understand the divine assistance given him accounts for his failure to understand why he must sacrifice, and his inability to actively redeem his personal past by trying to love accounts for his failure to understand the divine assistance.

Just as the redemption of the personal past involves more than the personal past (Part II of "The Dry Salvages"), so the acceptance of "Adam's curse" unites all men. Just as the lost moment in the rose-garden can be known only in time, which if allowed to become an endless cycle of meaningless experience, removes man further away from the still point, so the Incarnation can be known only in time and can easily become the lost Word again. Time is both a destroyer and a preserver of the lost moment and the Word in the memory. Life is a never-ending cycle, for "most of us," of active purgation, which allows us to redeem the personal past and, therefore, to rediscover the Incarnation, which redeems all of history (Part V of "The Dry Salvages"). This perennial cycle of redeeming the personal past is a constant death of the old life and a new beginning in life, which, in its intersection of the Incarnation, is a symbolic death of the senses and a rebirth of the spirit.

The spiritual life never leaves the stage of active purgation, despite its periodic pointing toward a higher stage, because "most of us" must constantly work at the rediscovery of the Incarnation. The spiritual life is cyclical because contemporary man's life is cyclical. Where Hopkins' speaker purges his senses so that he can be better prepared for the more intense purgation of the spirit, Eliot's speaker purges his senses so that he can rediscover his past and the Incarnation. Since time alienates man from God, he must constantly begin again in time to reach the timeless. Where Hopkins is concerned with the progression of the spiritual life, Eliot is concerned with the rediscovery of the spiritual life. In this sense, Hart Crane in the first half of *The Bridge* is much closer to Eliot than to the others.

The plays following the *Four Quartets* are a putting into practice the conclusions of all of Eliot's previous work. The characters, except possibly Celia and Colby, are not destined for sainthood. They are involved in a redemption of their personal pasts, an active purgation of the vestiges of lust, and an active acquisition of the virtues of faith, hope, and charity. In the process they discover, or awaken to, the timeless reality of the spiritual world.

The Cocktail Party replies "to that question which the *Four Quartets* left unanswered—What is the status of those people who are unable to attain self-abnegation and complete religious fulfillment . . . ?" [19] At the beginning of the scene between Edward and Sir Henry Harcourt-Reilly in the consulting room, the latter tells Edward that he still has "the chance of redeeming from ruin" two lives, his and his wife's (II). Redemption includes detachment from each other and each one's involvement with the past, resignation "to be the fool you are" (I.i), humiliation of having others know of the separation, and admission of the lust in the past. Both Edward and Lavinia must admit to themselves that their extra-marital affairs were devoid of love and were motivated by a failure to love each other, a failure to understand each other. They were blind to the fact that not trying to love each other, they would only perpetuate a lack of love with others. This admission is a purgation for them.

Arriving at the state of the speaker in *Ash Wednesday*— "Then what can we do / When we can go neither back nor forward?" (II)—they elect to try to understand each other and to make a more meaningful marriage; that is, they elect to have faith and hope. Edward's statement, "I'm beginning to feel very sorry for you, Lavinia" (II), is the commencement of charity. Once they understand how they failed each other and why they turned to Celia and Peter and why those relationships were of the nature of lust, not love, as their marriage was, they are on the way toward redeeming the past and preparing for a better future. Within the framework of the human condition, they are successful. They do make a new beginning. The ending of the play makes it apparent that theirs is to be a lifetime of active purgation of a sort in that they must work at understanding and loving each other.

Celia is destined for a richer spiritual life. She is, according to "The Dry Salvages," someone who is occupied at being a "saint." The "something given / And taken, in a lifetime's death in love" (Part V of "The Dry Salvages") indicates that the higher the progression of the spiritual life, the more grace one receives. Celia possesses two qualities which make her different from the others, "an awareness of solitude" and "a sense of sin," and she has awakened, made clear in her request "to be cured / Of a craving for something I cannot find / And of the shame of never finding it" (II). Her goal is the possibility of illumination and union (II). What is significant for this study is that we do not know if she ever reaches the intensity of the "terrible" sonnets, for Eliot solves the problem of spiritual growth beyond the beginning stage by having it occur on the island of Kinkanja. All we know is that Celia suffers and dies, "crucified / Very near an ant-hill" (III). The *Cocktail Party* is really dramatizing Harcourt-Reilly's summation, "Only by acceptance / Of the past will you alter its meaning" (III), for "most of us," those not engaged in the "occupation for the saint."

In *The Confidential Clerk* the redemption of the past involves determining who are one's parents and children. While probing into the past, Sir Claude and Lady Elizabeth speak honestly to each other about what each wanted to be and how each failed to understand the other (III). By the end of the play these two and Kaghan and Lucasta are resolved to work at love and understanding. The progression of the spiritual life is merely a possibility. It may be that Colby is destined for a more intense spiritual life than the others, for Lucasta tells him, "You're terribly cold. Or else you've some fire / To warm you, that isn't the same kind of fire / That warms other people" (III), but we know only that he leaves to be an organist in Joshua Park. If the other vocation suggested by Eggerson is more than "a stepping-stone / To a precentorship! And a canonry!" (III) we do not know. It is outside the play.

In *The Elder Statesman* certain expressions, images, motifs from Eliot's earlier work are found in a completely secular frame of reference, which indicates, of course, the initial degree of spiritual unawareness of the characters. Lord Claverton complains of the "fear of the emptiness before me" (I), not St. John of the Cross' emptying of all that is not God. When Gomez says to him, "You've changed your name twice —by easy stages, / And each step was merely a step up the ladder" (I), he means the social ladder, not the stairway in *Ash Wednesday* or the ten stairs in "Burnt Norton." Mrs. Carghill tells him, "You touched my soul— / Pawed it, perhaps, and the touch still lingers. / And I've touched yours" (II); these are human touches, not divine touches leading the soul into the illuminative stage. When Lord Claverton wishes Michael

> had some aim of high achievement,
> Some dream of excellence, how gladly would I help you!
> Even though it carried you away from me forever
> To suffer the monotonous sun of the tropics
> Or shiver in the northern night (II),

he does not mean the destination of Harry or Celia. By temporarily detaching himself from the past and confessing his sins of the past, Lord Claverton finds freedom: "I feel at peace now" (III). Accepting the truth of the past, he makes a new beginning: "I've been freed from the self that pretends to be someone; / And in becoming no one, I begin to live" (III).

The movement through purgation and redemption of the personal past brings the characters to the discovery of the timeless reality of the spiritual world. Following the announcement of Celia's death, Lavinia, who has made a new beginning, tells Peter, "You've only just begun. / I mean, this only brings you to the point / At which you *must* begin" (III). Near the end of the play, Edward realizes "that every moment is a fresh beginning" (III), and we should not forget that after Agatha reveals the past to Harry, which prompts him to say, "This is like an end," she replies, "And a beginning" (II.ii). Colby speaks of finding his father, "a dead obscure man" (III). To Sir Claude he says, "I must follow my father—so that I may come to know him" (III). Following Lord Claverton's acceptance of the past, which brings Monica and Charles closer together, she calls out, "Oh Father, Father! / I could speak to you now" (III). Lord Claverton dies under a beech tree, and the concluding words of the play are Monica's: "Now take me to my father."

V

Hart Crane

In the judgment of the 30's and the 40's, Hart Crane's *The Bridge* is a failure from many points of view. [1] Studying the poem from new perspectives, criticism of the 50's and the 60's finds it much more unified than does the earlier criticism. [2] But even though the later criticism finds structure and coherence established by the theme of the poem, the mythical and mystical quest, and even though critics comment on certain mystical elements, there has been relatively little detailed analysis of the total mystical-religious meaning of *The Bridge.* Yet Crane "was a mystic and in some sense a pantheist. He was religious in his approach to his art. He conceives of his greatest poem as an attempt to give America a religious epic." [3]

Although Crane appreciated the work of the other three authors, [4] his spiritual affinities are not with them. He is outside of the Roman Catholic tradition, and while close to Eliot in emphasizing the discovery of the spiritual life, he rejected the pessimism he saw in the poetry prior to *Ash Wednesday* (1/5/1923). We get an insight into the type of spiritual experience in *The Bridge* by noting revealing comments in his letters. To Yvor Winters he declares his interest in recording certain sensations which "approximate a true record of such moments of 'illumination' as are occasionally possible" (5/29/1927). To Gorham Munson he relates an experience "in the dentist's chair when under the influence of aether and *amnesia* my mind spiraled to a kind of seventh heaven of consciousness. . . ." (6/18/1922) To Waldo Frank he tells his understanding of the "Word made Flesh" (4/21/1924),[5] and to Charlotte Rychtarik he defines his idea of God: "The true idea of God is the only thing that can give happiness,—and that is the identification of yourself with *all of life*" (7/21/1923).

Crane gives aesthetic form to a kind of spiritual life radically different from that examined in the preceding chapters. And although Frank, one of Crane's closest friends, considers him a mystic,[6] I do not. I follow the commentators used in the previous chapters. The words *mystic* and *mystical*, however, will be used in this chapter for these two reasons: his poetry is mystical in the popular sense in that it contains a suspension of the rational faculties, a heightening of perception, and a suspension of the experience of time and space; and Crane uses the words to refer to his work. Whenever these words are used in relation to his poem, though, they will mean always *Crane's sense of mysticism.* Having used *pseudo-mystical* to designate Hopkins' early poems, I do not want to repeat it here. There is a spiritual insincerity in the early Hopkins; I defined it as an attempt to simulate or reproduce the mystic way. I do not consider Crane a mystical poet, but I do not question the integrity of the poem. I do not doubt that Crane believed in his kind of spiritual experience. Where the three degrees of beginners, proficients, and perfect do not apply, therefore, to the scheme of *The Bridge*, Miss Underhill's schematization will because it is more inclusive than the teachings of the tradition of which Hopkins is a part. We can turn to Rudolf Otto, who, more than St. Ignatius or St. John of the Cross or Fr. Garrigou-Lagrange, can help us to understand what Crane is doing. Mysticism, he writes, "while sharing the nature of religion . . . shows a preponderance of its non-rational elements and an over-stressing of them in respect to the 'over-abounding' aspect of the 'numen.' " [7]

That the poem has mystical elements is accepted; that it contains a large element of the non-rational is recognized. That the poem is a narrative of the fivefold division of the spiritual life and is concerned with the state of religion in contemporary life and with the possibilities of a spiritual life for modern man this chapter will demonstrate. The mystical-religious elements of the poem, attested to in Crane's letters (2/18/1923 and 3/18/1926), crystallize in six sections: "Proem: To Brooklyn Bridge," "Ave Maria," "The Dance," "Cape Hatteras," "The Tunnel," and "Atlantis." It must be pointed out here, because it helps to chart the spiritual progression, that in these sections there is a shift in verb form to the archaic second person singular, *thou est.*

"Ave Maria" and "The Dance" should be studied together as part of the first half; "Cape Hatteras" and "The Tunnel," as part of the second half. "Proem: To Brooklyn Bridge" establishes a religious frame of reference. After the secular images of the first three stanzas, the bridge is addressed as "Thee" in the fourth stanza, which may indicate that Crane is deifying it, although Rosenthal notes that the line containing "As though the sun took step of thee" suggests "an as-if divinity only." [8] In the seventh stanza we read that the "guerdon" of the bridge is "obscure as that heaven of the Jews"; nevertheless, "Accolade thou dost bestow / Of anonymity time cannot raise: / Vibrant reprieve and pardon thou dost show." Stanza seven of the "Proem" gives the first occurrence of the verb form change and sets up the religious frame of reference of the poem, which receives considerable support in the next two stanzas: "harp and altar," "choiring strings," "prophet's pledge," "prayer of pariah," "lover's cry," "immaculate sigh of stars," "beading thy path," and "condense eternity." The final stanza is a plea to the bridge:

> O Sleepless as the river under thee,
> Vaulting the sea, the prairies' dreaming sod,
> Unto us lowliest sometime sweep, descend
> And of the curveship lend a myth to God.

We must investigate the next section, "Ave Maria," and then return to the line, "And of the curveship lend a myth to God."

"Ave Maria" presents the second and third verb form shifts and the first epiphany. The third shift begins with the lines, "O Thou who sleepest on Thyself, apart / Like ocean athwart lanes of death and birth." The God, both masterful and merciful, praised in "Te Deum laudamus," the chief hymn of rejoicing in the Roman Catholic Church, is the God of medieval Christianity. This epiphany occurs near the Old World, the world of Roman Catholic Spain. God becomes manifest in fire (Exod. iii) in the Old World. In the New World the imagery begins with "Slowly the sun's red caravel drops light / Once more behind us. . . . It is morning there" and "I, wonder-breathing, kept the watch,—saw / The first palm chevron the first lighted hill," both passages implying that He is revealed in the New World, not in fire, but in light, which is not so intensely localized as fire. The presence of the medieval Christian God is not so keenly felt in the New World; the religion transported to the New World by Columbus undergoes a transmutation. The imagery continues to describe the physical universe and then moves through the sign that guides Columbus, "Who sendest greeting by the corposant, / And Teneriffe's garnet—flamed it in a cloud," through the diffusion of God's presence in an epiphany, "round thy brows unhooded now / —The kindled Crown," to the climactic ending of this section.

"Ave Maria" implies that God appears to Columbus in the New World and in the Old World partly because he has faith in "Madre Maria" (the second verb shift) and partly because he has faith in science, the science of navigation, in the stanza beginning, "Of all that amplitude that time explores." Crane's selection of "Elohim" provides a continuity with earlier religion, in this case, Judaism. ("Sapphire wheel" from this stanza recalls the visions in Ezek. i.) Two, it hints at the rational character of medieval Christianity:

> But what distinguishes Yahweh from El-Shaddai-Elohim is not that the former is an "anima," but (and the distinction may be applied to differentiate all god-types) that, whereas in Yahweh the numinous preponderates over the familiar "rational" character, in Elohim the rational aspect outweighs the numinous. "Outweighs" is as much as we can say, for in Elohim too the numinous element is certainly present; Elohim is, for instance, the subject of the genuinely numinous narrative of the theophany in the burning bush, with the characteristic verse (Exod. iii.6): "And Moses hid his face; for he was afraid to look upon God." [9]

By selecting "Elohim," a plural form, Crane may also be prefiguring the pantheism that will be dominant later in the poem.

Since "To Brooklyn Bridge" is an introduction to the entire poem, the "Proem" and "Ave Maria" complement each other. In "Ave Maria" faith and science lead Columbus to an epiphany of the Christian God, in which He becomes manifest in fire, and to a mystical experience (in Crane's sense) in which He is experienced as light. In the "Proem" faith in the concrete curve of the Brooklyn Bridge and in the pure curve it symbolizes can lead the protagonist to God. Faith and science can create a myth in which God is realized: "And of the curveship lend a myth to God." Crane once wrote, "The very idea of a bridge, of course, is a form peculiarly dependent on such spiritual convictions. It is an act of faith besides being a communication" (6/20/1926). Together, faith and science enable the protagonist to transcend merely applied science—"Till elevators drop us from our day"—and to realize God (2/18/1923).

There are two approaches to studying the first half of *The Bridge*, both of which are necessary for a complete understanding of the poem. The first is to take the sections in the order in which they appear, which is the order of the first three stages of the spiritual life. "The Harbor Dawn" is the awakening stage. The protagonist is visited by "a tide of voices" which "insistently through sleep" awakens him. His "eyes wide, undoubtful / dark / drink the dawn." Crane's marginal gloss, "recalls you to your love, there in a waking dream to merge your seed," shows that this is an example of the type of conversion in which the

> self awakes to that which is within, rather than to that which is without: to the immanent not the transcendent God, to the personal not the cosmic relation. Where those who look out receive the revelation of Divine Beauty, those who look in receive rather the wound of Divine Love....[10]

Fully awakened, he begins the quest in "Van Winkle."

In *The Bridge* the purification stage consists of detachment and mortification. The first, with its virtues of poverty, chastity, and obedience—found in the protagonist and then in the hoboes, the river, and the soil—is the quest for the mystic past in "Van Winkle," "The River," and the opening of "The Dance." The second, the killing of the senses, desires, and cravings, is the death at the stake ritual in "The Dance." The protagonist must temporarily detach himself from the twentieth century to discover the spiritual force that makes the twentieth century possible. We can understand this stage in Crane's poem if we remember that for him "the true idea of God ... is the identification of yourself with *all of life*," and, to anticipate what will be discussed later in this chapter, life in this world is a constant process of becoming, a never-ending process of transmutation. The protagonist's spiritual predicament is the result of his acceptance of only a *part of life;* he cannot grow spiritually because, denying the possibility of the spiritual life in the twentieth century, he has lost contact with the permanent spiritual force that is reflected in the changing present of any given time span. It is only by temporarily detaching himself from the present and mortifying his attachments to the present that he can discover the past—Dembo very effectively makes the point that the mythic past lies just beneath the surface, waiting to be rediscovered [11]—and his spiritual nature.

We can approach this consideration from another direction. For Hopkins, man's sin is the assertion of his will contrary to or independent of God's will. Purgation teaches humility and self-abnegation, admission that man is totally dependent on his Creator. Mortal beauty has its attraction and its limits: "Yea, wish that though, wish all, God's better beauty, grace." For Eliot, man's sin is the assertion of his will which results in lust. Purgation teaches humility which, with God's grace, makes human love possible. Life is redeemed through purgation. For Crane, man loses his spiritual potentialities when he denies life because it is ugly and materialistic, not realizing it is ugly and materialistic because he has denied its spiritual possibilities. That which is outside himself, whether it be mortal beauty or the world of nature or the world of artifacts, is also spiritual since it contains God. Although these comments about Crane's position will be qualified in the course of this study, it can be stated at this point that for Crane man is regenerated when he elects to be spiritual. Purgation allows the protagonist to temporarily withdraw from the life he rejects to discover his own spiritual nature—the awakening in the first stage is to that which is within—which, in turn, makes it possible for him to discover the spiritual substratum of all of life. He can then discover the spiritual basis of that which was thought to be ugly and materialistic.

The illuminative stage is the second half of "The Dance," consisting of the heightening of the protagonist's perception (stanzas 16, 17, and 18), the suspending of his experience of time and space (stanzas 19 and 20), and the merging with the Indian Brave (stanza 26). For the protagonist, in stanzas 21 through 25, the universe is transformed, made brilliant by its divinity. He has not yet achieved union, but he has become one with his past. It remains for him to become one with his present so that he can thrust himself into the future or, to look at it another way, it remains for him to achieve union with the spiritual force working itself out in the universe so that he can feel his sense of continuity with *all of life*: past, present, and future.

So far, we have been studying the first half of *The Bridge* in logical order. Since this chapter will attempt to show that much of the meaning of the first half has to do with the evolution of religious myth, it is necessary that we also study it in chronological order (9/12/1927). In "The Dance," the first section since "Ave Maria" to have the verb form shift (stanzas 21 and 22), the religion of the Indian, symbolized by the star, is sacrificed to the white man's religion, brought by Columbus to the New World and symbolized in the Old World by fire. The Indian's religious myth is subsumed under Christianity. The early stanzas of "The Dance" epitomize this entire section. Stanzas six and seven employ a star as symbol. The protagonist

> saw that fleet young crescent die,—
>
> And one star, swinging, take its place, alone,
> Cupped in the larches of the mountain pass—
> Until, immortally, it bled into the dawn.

109

In "The Dance" the Indian is sacrificed and merges with Pocahontas, "the mythological nature-symbol chosen to represent the physical body of the continent, or the soil" (9/12/1927). The "crescent" of the above stanza recalls the "crescent ring" of "Ave Maria," just as the star as sign recalls a similar star as sign to the Magi in Matt. ii. Christianity is becoming Indian animism, at the same time that the Indian religion is being subsumed under Christianity, and the fire imagery is becoming light imagery. Also in the above stanza the assimilation of Christianity and animism becomes "the dawn." This transmutation of religious systems is prefigured earlier in "Ave Maria," where God's presence encircles the globe with fire, as is the transmutation of fire imagery prefigured earlier in "Ave Maria," in the contrast of fire-Old World with light-New World.

Immediately following the sacrifice of the Indian and in the latter half of "The River," pantheism (God as earth) comes to be dominant. Christianity has merged with the soil: "The Passion spreads in wide tongues, choked and slow, / Meeting the Gulf, hosannas silently below." The River Jordan, where Christ made manifest His divinity (Mark i), appears in a secular context (stanza 13).

God as the earth evolves too. The reasons are obvious: the mutilation of the soil in a search for gold and the eventual desertion of the soil in "Indiana" and the coming of the age of science and technology. In the opening lines of "The River," there is an ironic juxtaposition of "COMMERCE and the HOLYGHOST" and "WALLSTREET AND VIRGINBIRTH." Even "Jesus" becomes a kind of expletive-swearword, and the original fire imagery in "Ave Maria" is now "a headlight" and "the tail lights" of the 20th Century Limited. By the time of "Van Winkle" Christianity is a hazy memory: "Or is it the Sabbatical, unconscious smile / My mother almost brought me once from church / And once only, as I recall—?"

By the time of "The Harbor Dawn," the dawn of a new era, all that remains externally of primitive religion is a disappearing star: "Under the mistletoe of dreams, a star— / As though to join us at some distant hill— / Turns in the waking west and goes to sleep." It joins the old gods of "The River" and "The Dance." Fire becomes light, which, as Coffman notes, is symbolic of discovery, love, vision, and revelation. In fact, "the light of *The Bridge* is predominantly the light of dawn." [12] In "The Harbor Dawn," the section in the first half closest in time to the twentieth century, the protagonist's gradual awakening parallels the gradual spread of sunlight on the window: "The window goes blond slowly. Frostily clears." In this section dawn is intimately associated with love, an adumbration of "Atlantis." Then, too, the language of the religious frame of reference, most prevalent in "Ave Maria," becomes progressively more dissociated from Christianity through "The Dance" and "The River," through "Van Winkle" and "The Harbor Dawn," where "surplices" are linked with "gongs," "veils" with "signals" ("gongs," "wails," and "strum of fog horns"), and "blessèd" with the female and with "sirens," to the "Proem," where noon is a "rip-tooth of the sky's acetylene" (which suggests the tool of construction), "traffic lights" are the "immaculate sigh of stars," and the bridge is dissociated from the fire of the sun: "As though the sun took step of thee."

Just as the line "As though to join us at some distant hill" implies that the star of primitive religion is only an as-if divinity in the twentieth century, so does the line "As though the sun took step of thee" imply that Christianity has given way to the twentieth century, the age of "New thresholds, new anatomies!" ("The Wine Menagerie")

The first half of *The Bridge* is the conquest of time, accomplished by the gradual enlarging of the protagonist's spiritual consciousness of his relation to religion, history, and time. In "The River" the serpent becomes symbolic of time

111

and the eagle becomes symbolic of space: "Time like a serpent down her shoulder, dark, / And space, an eaglet's wing, laid on her hair." To the hoboes, who have retained the sense of the past (stanza 8), time and fire are related: "Time's rendings, time's blendings they construe / As final reckonings of fire and snow." The fire of "Ave Maria" moves through the serpent symbolism, traditionally the antithesis of the Christian God, of "The River," where the hobo "trod the fire down pensively," to "Van Winkle," where the serpent, also symbolic of pantheism because of its proximity to the earth, diminishes to a garter snake, a "sunning inch of unsuspecting fibre," which flashes "as clean as fire."

All of these elements—fire, Christianity, the star, animism, pantheism as God in the earth, the serpent, the eagle, time and space—are united in "The Dance." The protagonist's consciousness is enlarged so that he participates in the Indian's experience, the last line of which section unites "the serpent with the eagle." The protagonist discovers that Judaism, Christianity, animism, God as the earth, and the dawn are all united, are all one. He has conquered time and space. By discovering "the physical body of the continent, or the soil," he knows that religion, history, and culture are evolutionary. Each stage of history grows out of the preceding stage, and each stage assimilates the preceding one. Fire becomes light becomes dawn. Elohim, Hebrew for God, becomes the Christian God becomes Love. "The bridge in becoming a ship, a world, a woman, a tremendous harp (as it does finally) seems to really have a career" (1/18/1926). The many of the temporal, spatial world are one—at least in the past. And the way to bridge the gap between the worlds of the Brave and the protagonist is through the mystical experience, each one of which enlarges and develops the protagonist's spiritual consciousness and prepares him for future mystical experiences. In the epiphany of the God of medieval Christianity as a Hand of Fire and the experience of Him as light in "Ave Maria," for Columbus the finite is united with the infinite; in the mystical experience in "The Dance," for the Brave the finite is united with the infinite. (The Indian achieves union; the protagonist, illumination.)

Both "Ave Maria" and "The Dance" present mystical-religious experiences. "Ave Maria" embodies an epiphany (theophany), a manifestation of the transcendent Reality. Concomitant with this manifestation are a suspension of the experience of time and space and a heightening of perception. In "Ave Maria" the God of medieval Christianity becomes a felt, living presence; He appears as fire; His presence brilliantly illuminates the heavens; His appearance causes "meridians [to] reel." The major difference between this section and "The Dance" is in the manifestation. In "Ave Maria" the emphasis is on the transcendent God who dominates the universe and gives meaning to Columbus' quest. The elements of what Otto designates the numinous experience are present: Columbus experiences feeling of awefulness, overpoweringness, energy, "wholly other," and fascination. There is a stillness and then there is a sense of gradually expanding rapture on the part of Columbus; he experiences a sense of creaturehood before the majestic God.

"The Dance" is more a mystical experience (in Crane's sense) than an epiphany. There is the suspension of the protagonist's experience of time and space, and there is the heightening of his perception. [13] The culmination of this section is the mystical illumination: "We danced, O Brave, we danced beyond their farms, / In cobalt desert closures made our vows. . . ." In contrast with "Ave Maria," "The Dance" is characterized by motion, speed, intoxication, and frenzy. The emphasis is on the subjective state of the protagonist in his quest:

> I left the village for dogwood. By the canoe
> Tugging below the mill-race, I could see

Your hair's keen crescent running, and the blue
First moth of evening take wing stealthily.

The focus is on the protagonist, who loses himself to find himself, to discover his identity and his relationship with time, space, and the mythic past.

We can appreciate the unity of *The Bridge* if, before turning to the second half of the poem, we pause to note books which Crane read and in which he could have encountered material that coincided with his own beliefs. When we put these fragments together, we can understand what takes place in the second half. In Whitehead's *Science and the Modern World* (3/5/1926), the impact of science on man's "metaphysical presuppositions," [14] the conflict between religion and science, and the evolution of religion, modifying itself according to advances in science. In Ouspensky's *Tertium Organum* (2/15/1923), the inability of science alone to answer to man's spiritual needs and the inevitable triumph of mysticism: "Nevertheless, *science must come to mysticism*, because in mysticism there is a new method—and then to the study of different forms of consciousness, i.e., of forms of receptivity different from our own. Science should throw off almost everything old and should start afresh with a new theory of knowledge." [15] In Frank's *Our America* (4/13/1923), the necessity of the mystic's vision—Whitman was one of "the great mystics" [16]—in rescuing America from its spiritual bankruptcy. Finally, in Frank's *Virgin Spain* (3/5/1926), a work we shall have occasion to look at again, the importance of Columbus, who in "his historic rôle belongs with the Spanish mystics" and who, in discovering America, provided an outlet for the energy generated by the dissolution of medieval Christendom. [17]

Together, these fragments form a coherent basis for *The Bridge*. The collapse of the unity of the medieval world and the advance of science have altered man's receptivity to

God. The medieval world has been assimilated into subsequent periods but, as the first part of the poem makes clear, the past has become submerged and must be rediscovered in the present before the mystical quest can continue. By itself, science, which is winning in its conflict with religion, leads to materialism. Denying man's spiritual life by assenting solely to materialistic values, America has substituted for the dawn of God, the taillights of the 20th Century Limited. The question facing Crane is how can contemporary man regain his lost faith, or how can Columbus' vision be redeemed?

In "Ave Maria" there are the epiphany in the Old World and the mystical experience in the New World: God manifested as a "Hand of Fire," rationally apprehended as "Elohim," and praised in "Te Deum laudamus" and God experienced as the dawn. What is crucial to the poem is that Columbus experiences both precisely because his mystic vision achieves a harmony of faith and science. He is a man of faith and a man of science. The solution to contemporary man's predicament, therefore, is to duplicate Columbus' vision. Just as Columbus bridges two worlds (the Old and the New, the epiphany and the mystical experience, the one and the many), so can man in the twentieth century bridge the two worlds of the one and the many through the union of faith and science.

There are two reasons, then, why Crane must continue if *The Bridge* is to be a unified, coherent work. One, the protagonist must test his illumination, which unites him to the past, in the quotidian world of the present. Two, the goal of the true mystic is the unitive way. In order to achieve the fifth stage, the protagonist must journey the dark night of the soul, the fourth stage. "Therefore the great seekers for reality are not as a rule long delayed by the exalted joys of Illumination. Intensely aware now of the Absolute Whom they adore, they are aware too that though known He is unachieved."[18]

"Ave Maria" presents the coming of Christianity to America; "The Dance," the subsuming of Indian animism under Christianity; "The River," the transmuting of Christianity and the assimilated Indian religion into pantheism as God in the earth; "Van Winkle" and the "The Harbor Dawn," the moving on to a new level of spiritual reality. (This summary is deceiving because the process of transmutation is endless. It is almost impossible to pinpoint when any one begins to be dominant.) We must conclude that between "Ave Maria" and "The Harbor Dawn" God can be experienced, for the one whose spiritual consciousness is properly enlarged and developed, in the Indian, the soil, the Mississippi Valley, the Mississippi River, the 20th Century Limited, and the dawn. The last line of the "Proem," "And of the curveship lend a myth to God," must refer to the creation of a religious myth to God, but not as the rationally apprehended and numinously experienced God of medieval Christianity who appeared in the unified and meaningful universe of Columbus and Who was responsible for the unity and meaning of that universe. He (or It, the spiritual force, since by God, Crane means *all of life*) must be experienced in other forms in the twentieth century.

The protagonist sets out on his quest for God in the world of the twentieth century. He must learn if this spiritual force can be experienced in the world of steel and jazz, resorts and dance halls. In "Cape Hatteras" he turns to the twentieth-century's finest achievement in time and space, the new physics and mathematics, embodied in the airplane: "The nasal whine of power whips a new universe. . . ."[19] If God can be found anywhere in the modern world, it should be here, but he quickly realizes that the mystical union will not take place. The airplane as airplane, merely applied science, cannot conquer time and space as the epiphany and the mystical experience do:

> But that star-glistered salver of infinity,
> The circle, blind crucible of endless space,
> Is sluiced by motion,—subjugated never.

Despite the significant change in verb form, the first occurrence since "The Dance" and the fifth occurrence in the poem, in the passage beginning, "While Cetus-like, O thou Dirigible, enormous Lounger," despite the sprinkling of religious language—"The benediction of the shell's deep, sure reprieve"— and despite the reminder to the pilot that he has "a Sanskrit charge / To conjugate infinity's dim marge— / Anew," the airplane fails as a "bridge." It is shot down, in the lines beginning, "Now eagle-bright, now / quarry-hid, twist— / —ing, sink with." Doubting the possibility of union, the protagonist asks Whitman "if infinity / Be still the same as when you walked the beach / Near Paumanok."

Crane wrote to Munson that "the more I think about my *Bridge* poem the more thrilling its symbolical possibilities become, and since my reading of you and Frank (I recently bought *City Block*) I begin to feel myself directly connected with Whitman. I feel myself in currents that are positively awesome in their extent and possibilities" (3/2/1923). In the poem Whitman is a spiritual forefather because he journeyed the dark night of the soul and "passed that Barrier that none escapes— / But knows it leastwise as death-strife"; he experienced the mystical union. [20] Since his mystical vision encompasses America, he is valuable as a guide for the protagonist (7/13/1930). When the airplane is linked with this vision, it becomes symbolic of man's rebirth, his new relationship with the universe, in a passage with obvious religious symbolism:

And now, as launched in abysmal cupolas of space,
Toward endless terminals, Easters of speeding light—
Vast engines outward veering with seraphic grace
On clarion cylinders pass out of sight
To course that span of consciousness thou'st named
The Open Road—thy vision is reclaimed!
What heritage thou'st signalled to our hands!

Time and space, however, are not yet conquered in the world of the present. Crane is very careful to communicate that no mystical union takes place in "Cape Hatteras." The passage beginning, "Cowslip and shad-blow, flaked like tethered foam," is similar in structure to that of passages in "The Dance"—"Thewed of the levin, thunder-shod and lean" and "Totem and fire-gall, slumbering pyramid"—and similar in the mood of the "I" quest to that of "The Dance." Both sections increase in motion and intensity, but the passage in "Cape Hatteras" culminates in a momentary illumination of Whitman's eyes, not in union: *"Panis Angelicus!* Eyes tranquil with the blaze / Of love's own diametric gaze, of love's amaze!" Whitman is "not greatest thou,—not first, nor last," but he will be the protagonist's guide through the quotidian world: "No, never to let go / My hand / in yours, / Walt Whitman / so." "Afoot again," from the ending of this section, is proof that the airplane fails. Unlike Whitman, the protagonist has yet to experience the fourth stage of spiritual growth.

From this point on he moves further away from union. The more he seeks among the particulars of a debased society, the more his spiritual consciousness is diminished. In "Three Songs" and "Quaker Hill" the progress is toward despair. The movement of the second half of *The Bridge* is an upward-downward one. The airplane rises, is shot down, and rises again when linked with Whitman's vision. "Southern Cross" and "National Winter Garden" are successive downward movements, temporarily lifted by "Virginia."

In "Quaker Hill" occurs the protagonist's insight that breaks the pattern. The force of the meaning of his experience in "The Dance" begins to dawn on him: "But I must ask slain Iroquois to guide / Me farther than scalped Yankees knew to go." He begins to realize his relationship with the past (stanza 6). In understanding that he must extend his knowledge of this relationship to include the real world of the twentieth century, no matter how ugly and materialistic, he resolves to "shoulder the curse of sundered parentage," to accept his "birthright . . . / That unfolds a new destiny to fill. . . ." To the question, "Must we descend as worm's eye to construe / Our love of all we touch?" the answer is, "Yes."

In "Ave Maria" Columbus faces the raging elements and the terrors of the unknown; in "The Dance" both the Indian and the protagonist face the torture at the stake (stanza 17), and the Indian elects his destiny, "like one white meteor, sacrosanct and blent," prior to achieving union. It is not until "Quaker Hill," though, that the protagonist elects the pain of the death that leads to spiritual rebirth and union. He now knows that only suffering and mystic death, no matter how agonizing, can lead to salvation:

> Breaks us and saves, yes, breaks the heart, yet yields
> That patience that is armour and that shields
> Love from despair—when love foresees the end.

Since, in the symbolism of the dark night of the soul stage, the way down precedes the way up, this section ends with a breaking of the upward-downward pattern that achieves neither God nor the daemonic. The epigraph to *The Bridge*— "From going to and fro in the earth, / and from walking up and down in it"—Satan's answer to God's question, "Whence comest thou?" points the way to union. The protagonist's willingness to accept mystic death breaks the pattern. He descends to the horror of the daemonic in "The Tunnel" to rise to the ecstasy of union in "Atlantis."

This interpretation receives support from another direction. Columbus has faith in the Virgin, in "Ave Maria." Her color is blue—"thy mantle's ageless blue"—as it is in "The Blessed Virgin compared to the Air we Breathe," the *Portrait*, and *Ash Wednesday*. Just as God is experienced in different forms in different ages, so Mary's blue is transmuted, also, through "the blue / First moth of evening" in "The Dance"; the "yonder breast / Snow-silvered, sumac-stained or smoky blue" in "The River"; the "eyes' engaging blue" in "Indiana"; the hill, "blue-writ and odor-firm with violets," in "Cape Hatteras"; to "blue-eyed Mary" in "Virginia." [21] In "Southern Cross" the protagonist is not sure if she is "Eve! Magdalene! / or Mary, you?" In "National Winter Garden" Magdalene shows the way to death and rebirth:

> Yet, to the empty trapeze of your flesh,
> O Magdalene, each comes back to die alone.
> Then you, the burlesque of our lust—and faith,
> Lug us back lifeward—bone by infant bone.

In "Virginia"—"virgin in process of 'being built' " (8/12/1926) —the protagonist has a second awakening. To "blue-eyed Mary with the claret scarf," he calls out: "O Mary, leaning from the high wheat tower, / Let down your golden hair!" Dembo refers to Crane's technique in the following manner: "That is, the poet is to follow signs, manifestations of the Absolute, that will eventually lead him to the Absolute itself and later help him preserve his faith." [22] He is beginning to be receptive to the signs that will lead him to union, the first of which appears after the death in life-life in death symbolism. The twentieth-century's religious myth is in the process of being created. The modern counterpart to the Virgin Mary is the idealized office worker: "Cathedral Mary," or "Virginia."

In "The Tunnel," the subway, symbolic of the evil of a

materialistic society, is meant to be daemonic. This section contains a daemonic epiphany, that of Poe, who is best understood in contrast with Whitman, even though they are both Crane's spiritual forefathers. Whitman's eyes are "tranquil with the blaze / Of love's own diametric gaze, of love's amaze!" Poe's eyes are "like agate lanterns." Whitman "upward from the dead / . . . bringest tally, and a pact, new bound, / Of living brotherhood." Poe's truncated "head is swinging from the swollen strap." His "body smokes along the bitten rails." I assume that by this Crane means that despite Poe's concern with man's spiritual life, his work lacks the completed experience. That is, I assume that the answer to the following question is Yes, that Poe did deny the ticket, did reject the dark night stage:

> And when they dragged your retching flesh,
> Your trembling hands that night through Baltimore—
> That last night on the ballot rounds, did you
> Shaking, did you deny the ticket, Poe?

Yet he shows the protagonist the way he must go.

The critics of the 30's and the 40's who saw in the ending of "The Tunnel" Crane's lack of faith in *The Bridge* failed to read the poem as a narrative of the mystic way and failed to understand the function of the daemonic epiphany, which, according to Otto, is essentially primitive and non-rational. This apprehension in the form of daemonic dread passes through a non-rational process of development until it rises to the level of holy awe of God. [23] The epiphany is successful: "And death, aloft,—gigantically down / Probing through you—toward me, O evermore!" By electing to ride the daemonic subway, by not denying the ostensible evil in contemporary society but by piercing through it to its spiritual substratum, the protagonist transmutes the materialistic into the spiritual. His spiritual consciousness is stirred to activity and affirmative movement again. Despair is conquered. The stanza preceding the one with the verb shift ends with "and straightway die!" The stanza beginning, "O caught like pennies beneath soot and steam, / Kiss of our agony thou gatherest," contains the first verb shift since "Cape Hatteras." The language and imagery are clearly religious; despite human frailty ("some song we fail to keep" —the song of "Quaker Hill"), the protagonist is reborn spiritually because he elects the mystic death of the fourth stage:

> And yet, like Lazarus, to feel the slope,
> The sod and billow breaking,—lifting ground,
> —A sound of waters bending astride the sky
> Unceasing with some Word that will not die...!

In a letter of March 20, 1926 to Waldo Frank, Crane praised *Virgin Spain*: "Just a word to say I have finished my first reading of your *Spain*. It is a book I shall go back to many times. Its magnificence and integrity are so rare that they constitute an embarrassment to our times in some ways. 'The Port of Columbus' is truly something of a prelude to my intentions for *The Bridge*...." In this section of Frank's book, Columbus tells Cervantes that the true New World will arise only after the destruction of the false New World in America. Their conversation continues:

> Cervantes—Look! Can't you see? . . . No! . . . God, the Towers are falling!
> Columbus—Glory to Jehovah!
> Cervantes—They veer, they twist. They have sunk in this mire of men.
> Columbus—The Seed shall rot.
> Cervantes—They are a turmoil of blind maggots. Their world is become as were their souls—a quicksand. The gleaming Towers are gone!

Columbus—Now shall be the birth of the World which
I discovered.
Cervantes—(*Sternly gazes west in a deep silence. Then
he turns to his friend.*) Gone is the city. Continents of chaos.
What shall rise?
Columbus—The Dream of the Old World, at last—a New
World! [24]

In "The Tunnel" the subway rises to the East River, to the
base of the Brooklyn Bridge, the concluding stanzas of the
"Proem." The memory of the illumination in "Powhatan's
Daughter" can be discarded in favor of the unitive life of
"Atlantis": "Here at the waters' edge the hands drop memory." "The Tunnel" concludes with a repetition of the symbolism of "Ave Maria"; here is the union of the epiphany of the
God of medieval Christianity and what will be the most
meaningful mystical experience for man in the twentieth
century.

"Atlantis," the fifth and final stage of the mystic way,
continues the upward movement that ends "The Tunnel":

Through the bound cable strands, the arching path
Upward, veering with light, the flight of strings,—
Taut miles of shuttling moonlight syncopate
The whispered rush, telepathy of wires.

All of the elements of the poem are synthesized in this section, which "is symphonic in including the convergence of all
the strands separately detailed in antecedent sections of the
poem—Columbus, conquests of water, land, etc., Pokahantus,
subways, offices, etc., etc." (1/18/1926) The pain and suffering of mystic death are conquered in spiritual rebirth; the
protagonist, "through smoking pyres of love and death, /
Searches the timeless laugh of mythic spears." The many of
the temporal, spatial world of becoming are united in the
non-temporal, non-spatial one, in the sixth stanza. There is

the significant verb shift, in the eighth stanza. There is a saturation of religious language and imagery, in the tenth stanza, for example. White is the dominant color, and fire imagery becomes brilliantly intensified again: "crystal-flooded aisle," "glistening fins of light," "blinding cables," and "radiance." In the final stanza Crane unites the basic symbol of the poem, the Bridge, with the form God took in the epiphany, Fire. The Bridge and Fire unite in the final "bridge" to God:

> So to thine Everpresence, beyond time,
> Like spears ensanguined of one tolling star
> That bleeds infinity—the orphic strings,
> Sidereal phalanxes, leap and converge:
> —One Song, one Bridge of Fire!

In the modern world the "Everpresence," which took the form of a "star" to the Indian, can be experienced in the Bridge's "orphic strings," which replace the "spears," the Indian's mode of experiencing God, yet which assimilate the "spears" in becoming "sidereal phalanxes."

In the penultimate stanza of "Atlantis," there occurs for the only time in the poem, a shift in verb form to the archaic third person singular:

> Migrations that must needs void memory,
> Inventions that cobblestone the heart,—
> Unspeakable Thou Bridge to Thee, O Love.
> Thy pardon for this history, whitest Flower,
> O Answerer of all,—Anemone,—
> Now while thy petals spend the suns about us, hold—
> (O Thou whose radiance doth inherit me)
> Atlantis,—hold thy floating singer late!

This stanza is the goal of the journey. The quest that begins in the "Proem" is completed in a mystical union that obliterates the suffering and alternating states of happiness and despair that precede it. For the protagonist Columbus' vision is redeemed in the quotidian world. In the language of Miss Underhill, which parallels Crane's, "the fully developed and completely conscious human soul can open as an anemone does, and *know* the ocean in which she is bathed." [25] In the "Proem" the "bridge" leads to "God"; in "Atlantis" the "bridge" leads to "Love." "God" is "Love."

Crane's letters—especially the well-known ones of January 5, 1923 to Munson; of February 18, 1923 to Munson; of March 18, 1926 to Kahn; and of February 27, 1923 to Frank —are indisputable proof that he saw in his art a hope for modern man. For Crane a religious myth can be constructed that will include steel and jazz, resorts and dance halls. There are, of course, two levels of meaning to the bridge: the bridge as Brooklyn Bridge, "the most superb piece of construction in the modern world" (5/11/1924), and the bridge as "bridge," symbol of the protagonist's gradually evolving consciousness and the means whereby he can experience the timeless in time. "Thus one might dare to say that *The Bridge* is not the Myth of America in an historical sense at all, but a construction and ritual celebration of the spiritual consciousness and creative force possible to America." [26] Two years before his death Crane was still confident about the meaning of his major work: "The poem, as a whole, is, I think, an affirmation of experience, and to that extent is 'positive' rather than 'negative' in the sense that *The Waste Land* is negative" (5/22/1930).

We can profitably contrast Eliot and Crane, a contrast the latter was well aware of.[27] Of the three other authors in this study, Eliot has certain general resemblances to Crane: both want to redeem the past; both utilize the memory; both are primarily concerned with the discovery of the spiritual life. But there are striking differences. In Part V of "The Dry Salvages," Eliot separates "the saint" from "most of us." It may be true that a person like Celia, with God's grace, will reach the illuminative stage or even the unitive stage, but the reader never knows for Celia's spiritual growth is outside of Eliot's writings. "Most of us" must work at purgation— "prayer, observance, discipline, thought and action"—so that we can redeem our pasts and awaken to the possibility of a transformed earthly life and spiritual growth. It is difficult enough to work at purgation and in so doing to become receptive to the "hint half guessed, the gift half understood," the "Incarnation." For Crane man's salvation lies in his developing and enlarging his spiritual consciousness so that he can experience the mystical union, and the union cannot occur until the protagonist grows through the four preceding stages. The past is not redeemed, Columbus' vision is not restored, science and religion are not brought into harmony until he elects the dark night stage. It is not enough, for Crane, to work a purgation alone; man must continually develop his receptivity to mystical experiences.

A second major difference is the non-existence of God's grace in *The Bridge*. In terms of the role of grace, Crane is at one extreme, Hopkins at the other, and Eliot in the middle. For Eliot man awakens to grace while he is trying to purge himself of his lust; while not denying grace, his poetry emphasizes man's activity. For Crane the exclusive responsibility is man's. The protagonist elects the dark night stage and, in so doing, experiences the mystical union. Union is not God-given. This is why Crane is not a mystical poet according to the definition given earlier in this study. The experience in *The Bridge*, which reaches frenzied heights in "The Dance" and "Atlantis," is the antithesis of the Christian experience. It is self-induced.

The Bridge, as the first part of this chapter has attempted to show, is a delineation of the decline of Christianity in the twentieth century. Images and symbols are dissociated from their traditionally religious meanings. The experience of Columbus is not possible in a world which lacks the structure and unifying principle of Columbus' world. In "Ave Maria" Columbus experienced an epiphany (theophany), but since this is the only epiphany in the poem—excluding the daemonic epiphany, whose function was discussed earlier—Crane is saying that God can no longer be apprehended and experienced in the terms of the medieval world. The age of science and technology has altered man's relationship with the universe and, consequently, man's relationship with God, or the spiritual force assuming different forms in different ages. The lines, "As though to join us at some distant hill," in "The Harbor Dawn," and "As though a god were issue of the strings," in "Atlantis," which imply an as-if divinity only, are evidence for the argument that the epiphany will not occur again. The modern world demands a modern religious myth.

For Crane modern man must cultivate the immanent Reality. This emphasis probably can be traced to Nietzsche's metaphysics: the denial of the transcendent realm ("God is dead"). The union of the serpent and the eagle that closes "The Dance" and "Atlantis" may allude to the serpent-eagle symbolism in the Prologue to *Thus Spoke Zarathustra*, where their union is the union of heaven and earth.[28] In any case, in "Ave Maria" God is not the ocean; God is "apart / Like ocean. . . ." He is the transcendent Reality, Who "dost search" between "lanes of death and birth." In the twentieth century it is man who must search for the immanent Reality; it is man who must elect the pain and suffering of mystic death that leads to spiritual rebirth. The mystic way is his salvation.

Answering "the commonest moral accusation against mysticism . . . that it functions in practice merely as an escape from the active duties of life into an emotional ecstasy of bliss which is then selfishly enjoyed for its own sake," Stace concludes that the "essential tendency of mysticism is therefore towards the moral life, the social life, the life of altruistic action, not away from these things." [29] "Cape Hatteras," "Quaker Hill," and "The Tunnel" are the strongest treatment of moral and social values in the poem. By developing and enlarging his spiritual consciousness, man will come to know that war, hatred, and violence—the airplane can be an instrument of destruction—because they violate the principle of Love, work contrary to man's spiritual needs. By developing and enlarging his spiritual consciousness, he will come to know that all men contain God, that all men can become united in their divinity. By developing and enlarging his spiritual consciousness, he will come to know that man is weak; it is the "curse" of his "birthright." Even though weak, he can be reborn. Once awakened, he can grow spiritually. The moral and social implications of this growth can contribute toward a spiritual rebirth in a world in which love is "a burnt match skating in a urinal."

Not only does each man contain divinity within himself, making all men partakers of God, the spiritual force, but since the world of the many is united in the one, the prosaic, the sordid, and the ugly objects of this world also are transformed into partakers of God. Hence the Brooklyn Bridge as basic symbol for the poem and the truth of Kloucek's statement: "Through the intricate symbolism of 'Atlantis' the protagonist is affirming that God exists in and through all things, and specifically that God exists in and through the things produced in modern man's industrial culture." [30] Of course, the irony in sections such as "The River" and "Cape Hatteras" and Crane's knowledge of man's reluctance to accept the necessity of spiritual growth prevent the poem from degenerating into a sentimental paean to progress or the author into a glib optimist.

We may disagree with the possibility of salvation offered in *The Bridge,* especially if our commitments are not to the type of spiritual experience Crane is writing about. We should credit him, however, with the creation of a unified, coherent poem that strikes directly at the core of the fundamental problem in the twentieth century, or in any century for that matter. It is also to his credit that, even though denying grace, he affirms man's responsibility for spiritual growth. Within its tradition *The Bridge* is an impressive testimony to man's spiritual potentialities.

VI

Conclusion

WE CAN CONCLUDE THIS STUDY BY NOTING EACH AUTHOR'S reaction to what is "the central fact of modern history in the West . . . the decline of religion." [1] One has only to think of other important authors such as Yeats, Stevens, Gide, Mann, Lawrence, Rilke, Camus, Kafka, Faulkner to see the value in determining a contemporary writer's relation to Christianity; the sense of spiritual homelessness, of spiritual rootlessness, is present in varying degrees in the works of these four men; the spiritual life, the structure of the works examined, is intimately a part of the theology of the Mystical Body of Christ.

The significance of the two starting points of *The Bridge* has been analyzed: Christianity was a stage in the endless process of becoming in the temporal, spatial world, and in the twentieth century science and materialism are winning in the conflict with religion. Science builds the Brooklyn Bridge, but by the end of *The Bridge* modern man creates a "bridge" to God. The stages of the spiritual life enable him to discover the spiritual force permeating all of the universe; the man who grows spiritually transforms the Brooklyn Bridge into a "bridge." The spiritual life effects a harmony between religion and science and in so doing creates a modern religious myth, which, like Christianity, will be another stage in the process of becoming.

Crane's religious myth is non-Christian. It lacks the essence of Christianity: sin and guilt and repentance, the Incarnation, the Redemption, and God's grace. Furthermore, it contains an element of pantheism, defined by Dean Inge as "the identification of God with the totality of existence, the doctrine that the universe is the complete and only expression of the nature and life of God, who on this theory is only immanent and not transcendent." Inge continues:

> On this view, everything in the world belongs to the Being of God, who is manifested equally in everything. . . . It is inconsistent with any belief in *purpose*, either in the whole or in the parts. Evil, therefore, cannot exist for the sake of a higher good: it must be itself good. . . .
>
> We may also call pantheistic any system which regards the cosmic process as a real *becoming* of God. According to this theory, God comes to Himself, attains full self-consciousness, in the highest of His creatures, which are, as it were, the organs of His self-unfolding Personality.[2]

We have seen how Crane equates God with "the identification of yourself with *all of life*" and how this notion is worked out in the poem: through discovering his own spiritual nature and growing spiritually, the protagonist finds the spiritual substratum in all of life. Electing the mystic death, he discovers the good in the ostensible evil in the subway. We have also seen how the Bridge "in becoming a ship, a world, a woman, a tremendous harp" finally becomes a "bridge."

Yet the strength of the poem, from Crane's point of view, is this element of pantheism, for although his religious myth does not have a community united in the Mystical Body of Christ, it does offer the possibility of a community united through each individual's willingness to grow spiritually. The implication of the poem is that if each man elects to grow through the four stages of the spiritual life, he can discover God, the immanent Reality, in all of life—in himself, in all men, in all that is outside himself. If enough men elect to grow spiritually, there is still hope, however slim, that the modern world can be saved and a genuine human community restored. And since the temporal, spatial world is always in the process of becoming, man will always have to grow spiritually to discover God in himself and in the world at any given stage of becoming. Where Eliot's characters must always discover the spiritual life in a cyclical world, Crane's protagonist must always discover the means to penetrate to the spiritual force unfolding itself in the world of becoming.

Before turning to the other three authors, we should establish the two aspects of the Church:

> As these two aspects are found in Christ's humanity, they will also be found in the mystic perpetuation of that humanity which is the Church. The Church will likewise be an empirical thing and a mysterious reality.
>
> First, it will be an empirical, concrete, visible, tangible thing, like all human realities that prolong themselves in some form of continuation; for it is a human institution, a human society. And it is a society quite visibly and tangibly; its sociology and canon law can be written down. . . .
>
> Secondly, the Church will be an invisible reality: a life of thought, love, and grace that is infused into souls, a divinization and adoptive sonship which, in the unity of the only-begotten, incarnate Son is diffused throughout all mankind so deeply as to be inaccessible to natural consciousness, and which, in the depths thus reached, unifies mankind in itself and attaches it to God.[3]

Even though the two aspects "are indissolubly united in the Church, without on that account being identified," [4] either one can be emphasized more than the other. There are times in Eliot's poetry where the sense of the Church as the Mystical Body of Christ is strong: the anchorite praying "for the Church, the Body of Christ incarnate" in Chorus II from "The Rock"; the priest crying out to Thomas that the knights "come not like men, who / Respect the sanctuary, who kneel to the Body of Christ" in Part II of *Murder in the Cathedral;* the reminder that "the communication / Of the dead is tongued with fire beyond the language of the living" in Part I of "Little Gidding"; and the descent of the dove in Part IV of "Little Gidding." Usually, though, when we encounter the Church in his writings, especially in the prose, it is as "an empirical, concrete, visible, tangible thing," as "a human institution, a human society." This is the sense of the Church communicated in "The Humanism of Irving Babbitt," "Thoughts after Lambeth," *The Idea of a Christian Society,* and *Notes towards the Definition of Culture,* to name but a few pieces.

We do Eliot a serious injustice if we minimize such passages as the following: "To justify Christianity because it provides a foundation of morality, instead of showing the necessity of Christian morality from the truth of Christianity, is a very dangerous inversion. . . ." [5] Neither should we minimize his sense of the human community, united in "our, and Adam's curse" (Part IV of "East Coker"), and his sense of "communal responsibility, of the responsibility of every individual for the sins of the society to which he belongs." [6] But if we were to document every instance of the Church in his works and if we were to document the development of his thought and art from the first work through the last, we would find that he has always been seeking to uncover the cultural still point of the turning world. That the cultural still point is, in his later works, the Incarnation is another way of stating that Eliot has always been a man imbued with a deep religious sense.

In the chapter on Eliot I attempted to show that for him, unlike Hopkins, spiritual growth is of secondary importance. From the *Ariel Poems* and *Ash Wednesday* on, of primary importance is the discovery of the spiritual life, which allows for the possibility of a transformed earthly life and spiritual growth. Human love can be redeemed after the pride that produces lust is broken. In an attempt to indicate shades of emphasis, we might state that Eliot, unlike Hopkins, is more interested in affirming the necessity of the spiritual life than in spiritual growth beyond the purgative stage, the degree of beginners, and that Eliot, unlike Hopkins, is more interested in the Church as an institution in this world, the embodiment of Christianity, the standard by which we judge cultural, religious, ethical, legal, and social considerations than as the Mystical Body of Christ. This is not to imply that Eliot is more socially- and morally-minded than Hopkins, for they would agree that "since Christians are members of Christ, their sufferings are, if we may be allowed the term, member-sufferings. And every man is a member of Christ, at least in God's invitation. These member-sufferings are joined to the complete suffering of the Redeemer, and are means of union with Christ." [7] But, as we shall see, the aspect of the Church as an institution uniting men culturally is not stressed in Hopkins so much as is the aspect of men united in membership in Christ.

For Eliot, then, man's spiritual homelessness is the result of original sin and all that follows from it. This homelessness is intensified by living in a non-Christian world, a world in which "anything like Christian traditions transmitted from generation to generation within the family must disappear," [8] a world in which the sacramental and ritualistic life, which formerly made man aware of a transcendent realm, has been lost. It is only in a return to Christianity that the Western cultural tradition can be preserved; it is only in a return to Christianity that a continuity with the past can be maintained; it is only in a return to Christianity that Western man can find what was once, in the words of William Barrett, "the final and unquestioned home and asylum of his being";[9] it is only in a return to Christianity that there can be a genuine community for the West. Holroyd's conclusion is interesting:

> For, with the exception of Eliot, all our poets [Thomas, Whitman, Yeats, Rimbaud, Rilke] have been adamant individualists, in opposition against the established Church, and for the most part concurring with Thomas's view that Christianity is a "spent lie." It is true that "the great poet, in writing himself, writes his time," but both the selves and the time which these poets have documented have been chaotic, and, though they may have found their personal solutions to their predicament, these have invariably been invalid in the wider world. Eliot alone would have agreed with Father Zossima that "the true security is to be found in social solidarity rather than in isolated individual effort." [10]

Since Stephen Dedalus' spiritual development is inverted, it follows that his sense of the Mystical Body is inverted. Chapter III concludes with his receiving the sacrament of the Eucharist, "pre-eminently the sacrament of the Church and the mystical body, the sacrament of the Christian and of Christian life." [11] This should be a new life for him: "—*Corpus Domini nostri . . . —In vitam eternam. Amen*" (150). But not only are the last pages of this chapter presented ironically, as I showed in the chapter on Joyce, what is presented in the beginning of Chapter IV is also ironic.

This chapter opens with Stephen's inverted purgative stage. In view of his receiving the Eucharist in Chapter III and the particular grace produced by this sacrament, an increase of charity, the following passage in the midst of his purgation—"To merge his life in the common tide of other

135

lives was harder for him than any fasting or prayer . . ." (155) —can only be read as another example of his reversed and inverted spiritual life. His pride increases and he moves further away from the human community. He rejects the Blessed Virgin, the Christian Brothers, the students on the beach, the flower girl, the dean of studies, the students' petition *per pax universalis*, and so on.

Father Mersch explains that the Church consists of both body, the empirical society, and soul, "the factor that makes this society a living organism . . . the first general principle of a collective and unified life in all the members." [12] The soul of the Mystical Body is the Holy Ghost. By the end of Chapter IV Stephen has substituted his own mystical body. Watching the students on the beach who have "taken refuge in number and noise from the secret dread in their souls," he rejoices because "he, apart from them and in silence, remembered in what dread he stood of the mystery of his own body" (172-173). Two paragraphs later his body and soul are united in an "ecstasy of flight" (173). Red is traditionally associated with the descent of the Holy Ghost on Pentecost, symbolizing the tongues of fire. Stephen can "no longer quench the flame in his blood. He felt his cheeks aflame and his throat throbbing with song" (174). He comes upon the wading girl, whose "bosom was as a bird's, soft and slight, slight and soft as the breast of some darkplumaged dove" (175). This dove's image—"a faint flame trembled on her cheek" (176)—passes into his soul forever:

> He turned away from her suddenly and set off across the strand. His cheeks were aflame; his body was aglow; his limbs were trembling. On and on and on and on he strode, far out over the sands, singing wildly to the sea, crying to greet the advent of the life that had cried to him (176).

This advent prepares him for his awakening in Chapter V.

In Chapter V his rejection of the orthodox spiritual life and the Mystical Body of Christ is rapid and complete. He prefers Fortunatus' *Vexilla Regis prodeunt* over the hymn written by St. Thomas Aquinas for Maundy Thursday, beginning, *Pange lingua gloriosi corporis mysterium* (214); he can neither believe nor disbelieve in the Eucharist (243); he will not serve "my home, my fatherland, or my church" (251); he rejects the dead, members of the Mystical Body (252); and he "cannot repent" (253).

Since Stephen's spiritual life is the orthodox life reversed and inverted, the irony in the novel is inescapable. It ends with his discourse with himself, he is outside of the human community, he is caught in the nightmare of history, his mystical body contains a membership of one, and he is incapable of creating art. We are justified in concluding that he is a spiritually sick young man suffering from the deadliest of sins. By his own admission he cannot love (244), and it is difficult to believe that Joyce thought of the mature artist as a man incapable of love. In addition, Stephen's seeing himself as a type of the God-man is ironic, since Christ's assumption of human nature is the greatest of all acts of love.

There are in Hopkins' poetry passages that present the first aspect of the Church: in "Easter," "The Loss of the Eurydice," and "Andromeda," for example. And Hopkins, quite naturally, shares with Eliot and Crane a concern with the decline of religion ("Andromeda"). But this aspect receives slight treatment compared with that of the second aspect, membership in the Mystical Body of Christ.

Following Fr. Boyle, I have called attention to the Incarnation as the central fact in Hopkins' poetry. Because the Incarnation includes the Redemption and the Mystical Body as well, for the Mystical Body is the extension of the Incarnation, membership in Christ is also a central fact in his poetry. Through Christ the Word has come to dwell in all men, uniting all men in Him:

> Men here may draw like breath
> More Christ and baffle death;
> Who, born so, comes to be
> New self and nobler me
> In each one and each one
> More makes, when all is done,
> Both God's and Mary's Son (# 60).

The bugler in poem 47 is "realm both Christ is heir to and there reigns"; "Christ lived in Margaret Clitheroe"; the nun's sacrifice in *The Wreck* unites her in the Mystical Body and points the way for all mankind: "Let him easter in us."

Granted that the Incarnation is the central truth for each man, the Incarnation in Eliot's work is open to more interpretations than that of the Word made Flesh. Where Bodelsen takes "Incarnation" in "The Dry Salvages" in "its strict theological sense, viz. the Incarnation of Christ," [13] Holroyd, noting the missing definite article, takes it "in a general sense to mean the intersection of the timeless moment with time." [14] We cannot overlook the theological implications in the cyclical view of history in his writings and the efficacy of the grace that does not seem to assist man to break out of the cyclical pattern. There is not this ambiguity in Hopkins' work. In the sestet to poem 57, "the just man justices; / Keeps grace: that keeps all his goings graces; / Acts in God's eye what in God's eye he is— / Christ." Because, in the language of Father Mersch, "what Christ does, what He allows men to do with Him, is radically the full realization of what He is," [15] the poem concludes:

> for Christ plays in ten thousand places,
> Lovely in limbs, and lovely in eyes not his
> To the Father through the features of men's faces.

It follows from the truth of the Incarnation, Redemption, and Mystical Body that there is in Hopkins a sense of fellowship in Christ that we do not get in Eliot, a sense of compassion and charity that sees Christ's "youngster" in the bugler, the "child" in Felix Randal, "my mate and counterpart" in "every other / Man" (# 116).

The orthodox spiritual life, therefore, receives its fullest expression in Hopkins' poetry, even though it never reaches the final stage. All the stages are present in *The Bridge*, but there are philosophical and theological objections to the kind of spiritual experience in the poem. All the stages are present in the *Portrait*, too, but in a very special way. My thesis is not that Joyce is a defender of the Roman Catholic faith or the Church but that the structure of the novel as a reversed and inverted spiritual life explains Stephen at the end of the *Portrait* and the opening of *Ulysses*. Through the traditional progression of the spiritual life, Joyce can portray the moral and spiritual effects of pride.

To conclude that Hopkins' poetry best expresses the orthodox progression does not necessarily mean that he is the best artist in the group. To determine this would go outside the scope of this study. Neither is it a startling conclusion, given each man's biography. Nor am I particularly interested in proving that Hopkins is more orthodox than Crane. I attempted to take each artist on his own terms. What this study has demonstrated, I trust, is that the writings of four contemporary authors of major stature aesthetically embody the degrees, or ways, or stages, of the spiritual life and that their work reveals a greater depth of meaning when the four are studied in relation one to the other.

Footnotes

CHAPTER I

1. For an instance of this disagreement, see J. V. Bainvel's Introduction to A. Poulain, *The Graces of Interior Prayer,* trans. Leonora L. Yorke Smith (St. Louis, 1957), pp. lxxxvii-lxxxix.

2. *The Theology of the Spiritual Life,* trans. Paul Barrett (New York, 1953), pp. 10-11.

3. *An Introduction to the Study of Ascetical and Mystical Theology* (Milwaukee, 1957), p. 4.

4. *The Mystical Life* (St. Louis, 1956), p. 50.

5. *The Ascetical Life,* rev. ed. (St. Louis, 1955), p. 235.

6. Goodier, pp. 6-7.

7. "Hopkins and Donne: 'Mystic' and Metaphysical," *Ren,* IX (Summer, 1957), 180.

8. See David A. Downes, *Gerard Manley Hopkins* (New York, 1959), pp. 131-132; W. H. Gardner, Introduction to the *Poems,* 3rd ed., rev. (London, 1960), pp. xxv-xxvi; Geoffrey H. Hartman, *The Unmediated Vision* (New Haven, 1954), p. 54; Alan Heuser, *The Shaping Vision of Gerard Manley Hopkins* (London, 1958), p. vii; G. F. Lahey, *Gerard Manley Hopkins* (London, 1930), pp. 123, 142-143; and E. I. Watkins, *Poets and Mystics* (New York, 1953), p. 11.

9. Poulain, p. 1.

10. *Gerard Manley Hopkins* (London, 1942), p. 131.

11. *Christian Spirituality,* 4 vols; *Later Developments: Part I, From the Renaissance to Jansenism,* III, trans. W. H. Mitchell (Westminster, 1953), pp. 8-10.

12. *Western Mysticism* (New York, 1924), p. 31.

13. de Guibert, p. 267.

14. *Mysticism,* 12th ed., rev. (London, 1957), pp. 176-197.

15. See the work of Helen Gardner, Louis L. Martz, and Helen C. White. In *The Poetry of Meditation* (New Haven, 1954), Martz writes, "I believe there is a direct, a deliberate, relationship between poetry and meditation in the twentieth century," p. 326.

16. Georges Cattaui, *Trois Poëtes* (Paris, 1947); David Morris, *The Poetry of Gerard Manley Hopkins and T. S. Eliot in the Light of the Donne Tradition* (Bern, 1953); and Philip M. Martin, *Mastery and Mercy* (London, 1957).

17. *A New Approach to Joyce* (Berkeley, 1962), p. 18.

CHAPTER II

1. The fullest treatment of the early poetry as a unit is found in W. H. Gardner, *Gerard Manley Hopkins*, 2nd ed., rev., 2 vols. (London, 1961). Individual poems are treated in Robert Boyle, *Metaphor in Hopkins* (Chapel Hill, 1961); James Kissane, "Classical Echoes in Hopkins' 'Heaven-Haven,'" *MLN*, LXXIII (November, 1958), 491-492; and Boyd Litzinger, "The Genesis of Hopkins' 'Heaven-Haven,'" *VN*, No. 17 (Spring, 1960), 31-33, and "Hopkins' 'The Habit of Perfection,'" *Expl*, XVI (October, 1957), Item 1.

2. Underhill, p. 169.

3. *The Three Ages of the Interior Life*, trans. Sister M. Timothea Doyle, 2 vols. (St. Louis, 1960), I, 270-271. See Goodier, p. 142.

4. This early version of "Heaven-Haven" is found in *The Journals and Papers of Gerard Manley Hopkins*, ed. Humphry House and Graham Storey (London, 1959), p. 33.

5. *Mysticism and Philosophy* (New York, 1960), p. 132.

6. Underhill, p. 73.

7. Butler, pp. 160-161.

8. See Martz's careful distinction between "mystical" and "meditative," p. 20.

9. *The Journals*, p. 56.

10. *Ibid.*, pp. 58-59.

11. Downes' work is "a reading of G. M. Hopkins as a meditative poet" based on the "delineation of a tradition of meditative poetry," p. 10, as set forth in Martz's book. This approach has been used by others—Helen Gardner and Helen C. White—and with individual poems of Hopkins: for example, Alexander W. Allison, "Hopkins' 'I wake and feel the fell of dark,'" *Expl*, XVII (May, 1959), Item 54, and Sister Thérèse, "Hopkins' 'Spelt From Sibyl's Leaves,'" *Expl*, XVII (April, 1959), Item 45.

12. "Gerard Manley Hopkins: An Idiom of Desperation," *Proceedings of the British Academy*, XLV (1959), 179.

13. Underhill, p. 254.

14. A. A. Stephenson, "G. M. Hopkins and John Donne," *Downside Review*, LXXVII (Summer-Autumn, 1959), 301.

15. *The Journals*, pp. 71-72.

16. See Christopher Devlin, ed. *The Sermons and Devotional Writings of Gerard Manley Hopkins* (London, 1959), p. 107, and Hopkins' notes on the fifth exercise in *The Sermons*, pp. 137-138.

17. Fr. Boyle writes, "The life-giving power of divine life as it pours from the Heart of Christ, the ultimate significance of the Incarnation, is the basic key to all of Hopkins' mature work, as I see it," p. 195.

18. *The Letters of Gerard Manley Hopkins to Robert Bridges,* ed. C. C. Abbott, rev. ed. (London, 1955), p. 175.

19. *The Sermons*, p. 154.

20. See de Guibert, pp. 265-273; Garrigou-Lagrange, I, 267-470; Goodier, pp. 124-162; and Parente, *The Ascetical Life*, pp. 56-113.

21. Parente, *The Ascetical Life*, p. 115.

22. See de Guibert, pp. 273-282; Garrigou-Lagrange, II, 3-349; Goodier, pp. 162-186; and Parente, *The Ascetical Life*, pp. 113-135.

23. de Guibert, p. 281. See Garrigou-Lagrange, II, 117-140.

24. *The Sermons*, p. 254.

25. M. B. McNamee, "Mastery and Mercy in *The Wreck of the Deutschland*," *CE*, XXIII (January, 1962), 267.

CHAPTER III

1. The basic study of the structure is Hugh Kenner, "The *Portrait* in Perspective," in *James Joyce*, ed. Seon Givens (New York, 1948), pp. 132-174, and *Dublin's Joyce* (Bloomington, 1956), pp. 109-133. Studies that supplement it, disagree with it, or offer new directions are C. G. Anderson, "The Sacrificial Butter," *Accent*, XII (Winter, 1952), 3-13; Virginia D. Moseley, "James Joyce's 'Grave of Boyhood,'" *Ren*, XIII (Autumn, 1960), 10-20; Grant H. Redford, "The Role of Structure in Joyce's 'Portrait,'" *MFS*, IV (Spring, 1958), 21-30; Robert S. Ryf, *A New Approach to Joyce* (Berkeley, 1962); William York Tindall, *A Reader's Guide to James Joyce* (New York, 1960), pp. 50-100; and Dorothy Van Ghent, *The English Novel* (New York, 1953), pp. 263-276.

2. Underhill, pp. 178-179.

3. *Ibid.*, pp. 180-181.

4. *Ibid.*, p. 197.

5. For Miss Underhill on this stage, see pp. 198-231.

6. For Miss Underhill on this stage, see pp. 232-265.

7. For Miss Underhill on this stage, see pp. 380-412.

8. "The First Version of Joyce's 'Portrait,'" ed. Richard M. Kain and Robert E. Scholes, *YR*, XLIX (Spring, 1960), 362. See "The Bruno Philosophy," in *The Critical Writings of James Joyce*, ed. Ells-

worth Mason and Richard Ellmann (New York, 1959), p. 134, and the untitled, incomplete holograph manuscript, "William Blake," *ibid.,* p. 221.

9. Poulain, pp. 200-219.
10. For Miss Underhill on this stage, see pp. 413-443.
11. Richard Ellmann, *James Joyce* (New York, 1959), p. 2; Stanislaus Joyce, *My Brother's Keeper,* ed. Richard Ellmann (New York, 1958), p. 33; and Joyce himself by way of Francini Bruni, *Joyce Intimo Spogliato in Piazza* (Trieste, 1922), quoted in Ellmann, p. 226.
12. *A Reader's Guide,* p. 76.
13. "The Artist and the Rose," *UTQ,* XXVI (January, 1957), 185. See her *Symbolic Rose* (New York, 1960), pp. 187-202.
14. *Ibid.,* p. 186. This reads "inescapable echo of Dante" in *The Symbolic Rose,* p. 197.
15. *Stephen Hero,* ed. Theodore Spencer, John J. Slocum, and Herbert Cahoon (New York, 1955), p. 174. In the same passage he admits that "he was compelled to express his love a little ironically."
16. *My Brother's Keeper,* p. 7.
17. *James Joyce,* rev. and aug. ed. (Norfolk, 1960), p. 19.
18. "The Artist and the Rose," p. 185.
19. *My Brother's Keeper,* p. 33.
20. The nun in *The Wreck,* who calls, " 'O Christ, Christ, come quickly,' " causes the speaker to begin to examine his spiritual life. In Chapter V for Stephen the nun who cries out, "—Jesus! O Jesus! Jesus!" is "mad" (179).
21. Kenner, "The *Portrait* in Perspective," p. 170. This reads "which, with Ibsen's *Brand,* is the chief archetype of Joyce's book" in *Dublin's Joyce,* p. 130.
22. In addition to this instance the word *memory* occurs six times in the first ten pages of this chapter. This does not take into account words such as *recall* (179) and *remembering* (182), nor does this study document the frequency of the word *restless,* the key word in the most-quoted line from the *Confessions*: "Our heart is restless until it rests in you" (I.i).
23. In Book IX, Chapter 2, St. Augustine recalls that "because of too much literary work, my lungs had begun to weaken and it was difficult for me to breathe deeply. By pains in my chest they showed that they were injured, and it was impossible to make clear or extended use of my voice."
24. See Mark Schorer's judgment on the ending of the novel, "Technique as Discovery," in *Forms of Modern Fiction,* ed. William Van O'Connor (Minneapolis, 1948), p. 21.
25. Garrigou-Lagrange, I, 379.

26. In an unpubl. diss., "Epiphany and Dantean Correspondence in Joyce's *Dubliners*: A Study in Structure" (Syracuse, 1962), Stanley L. Jedynak presents a very convincing case for *accidia* (*acedia*), here meaning paralysis of the will, as the most pervasive of the deadly sins in *Dubliners*.

27. See "The noise . . . from others" (66); "The causes . . . insincerity" (69); "But when . . . loneliness" (70); "Stephen, though . . . number two" (75); "Any allusion . . . in a moment" (78); "You can't . . . sure five" (79); "Pride and hope . . . baffled desire" (89); "He listened . . . no pity" (90); "He recalled . . . of his mind" (94); "He could respond . . . father's voice" (95); "Stephen had tried . . . coughing" (96); "Stephen watched . . . of the moon" (98); and "He saw clearly . . . fosterbrother" (101).

28. At first glance the use of the *Dark Night* (the fourth stage) for Chapter IV (the second, or purgative, stage) may seem to be an error. One of the purposes of these chapters, however, is to remind the exercitant what he can do to remove these imperfections so that his soul may merit passive purgation (I.iii).

29. Kenner, "The *Portrait* in Perspective," pp. 164-165, and *Dublin's Joyce*, p. 126, applies the seven deadly sins to the opening of Chapter III.

30. See "A flame . . . proud musings" (161); "What had come . . . every order?" (164); "It was idle . . . as themselves" (170); "Like a scene . . . thingmote" (171); and "Their banter . . . proud sovereignty" (173).

31. Heb. v.1-6. Since St. Paul (Saul) was present at the martyrdom of St. Stephen, with whom Stephen identifies himself (253), it is almost inevitable that there should be allusions to his writings. Miss Moseley, "James Joyce's 'Grave of Boyhood,'" suggests Heb. ix.11-15.

32. 1 Cor. xiii.8-13. Kenner, "The *Portrait* in Perspective," p. 138, suggests 1 Cor. xiii.12 for "through a glass" in the second paragraph of the novel.

33. "James Joyce and the Hermetic Tradition," *JHI*, XV (January, 1954), 23-39; *The Literary Symbol* (New York, 1955), pp. 57-58; and *A Reader's Guide*, p. 82.

34. *The Rhetoric of Fiction* (Chicago, 1961), pp. 326-336.

35. Caroline Gordon, "Some Readings and Misreadings," *SR*, LXI (July-September, 1953), 388-389. Although I disagree with the severity of her judgment, I do agree with her when she writes that "his sin, pride, begets in him a terrible restlessness," in *How to Read a Novel* (New York, 1957), p. 212. J. Mitchell Morse, "The Artist as Savior," *MFS*, V (Summer, 1959), 103-107. See his *Sympathetic Alien* (New York, 1959). David Daiches, "James Joyce: The Artist as Exile," in *Forms of Modern Fiction*, ed. William Van O'Connor

(Minneapolis, 1948), p. 63. See his *Novel and the Modern World,*
rev. ed. (Chicago, 1960), pp. 83-90.

36. "A Portrait of the Artist as Beginner," *UKCR,* XXVI (March,
1960), 189.

37. Eugene M. Waith, "The Calling of Stephen Dedalus," *CE,*
XVIII (February, 1957), 256.

38. *James Joyce and the Making of "Ulysses,"* 2nd ed. (London,
1937), p. 61.

39. "Joyce and Stephen Dedalus: The Problem of Autobiography," in *A James Joyce Miscellany,* 2nd Ser., ed. Marvin Magalaner
(Carbondale, 1959), p. 71.

40. Throughout this study I have been referring to Dante, St.
Augustine, and St. John of the Cross as "sources." Should it be decided
that their works are not "sources" but, at best, "parallels" or "arche-
types" or "analogues" is not to cancel out this study. Set against the
Portrait, they illuminate it because they embody the traditional progression of the spiritual life. Although I am convinced that they are
"sources," I do not believe that Stephen's biography is taken *in toto*
from these works. Even though criticism that sees the *Portrait* as more
symbolic than naturalistic and the studies that examine scenes in the
novel as fusions of autobiography and literary allusion—for example,
Caroline G. Mercer, "Stephen Dedalus's Vision and Synge's Peasant
Girls," *NQ,* VII (December, 1960), 473-474—seriously weaken the
strict autobiographical interpretation, one cannot willfully and bla-
tantly ignore the facts of Joyce's life.

41. *A Reader's Guide,* p. 69.

CHAPTER IV

1. D. E. S. Maxwell, *The Poetry of T. S. Eliot* (London, 1958),
p. 150. There is a resemblance between my study and the one by
Elizabeth Drew, *T. S. Eliot* (New York, 1949). Witness this passage:
"All four of the [*Ariel*] poems embody different aspects of the experi-
ence of rebirth, of the discovery of a new focus of existence," p. 118.
The difference is that she is writing from a Jungean perspective.

2. Seán Lucy, *T. S. Eliot and the Idea of Tradition* (London,
1960), p. 156.

3. In this essay he observes that in Canto XXVI of the *Purgatorio*
the "souls in purgatory suffer because they *wish to suffer,* for purgation," in *Selected Essays,* new ed. (New York, 1950), p. 217, and
later in the same essay he gives his "prejudice that poetry not only
must be found *through* suffering but can find its material only *in*
suffering," p. 223.

4. *After Strange Gods* (New York, 1934), pp. 40-41.
5. *Selected Essays*, pp. 231-234.
6. F. O. Matthiessen, *The Achievement of T. S. Eliot*, 3rd ed. (New York, 1959), p. 116.
7. See Canon Martin, p. 144.
8. Parente, *The Mystical Life*, pp. 97-111.
9. Garrigou-Lagrange, I, 13-23.
10. Poulain, pp. 574-578.
11. Garrigou-Lagrange, I, 24.
12. Friedrich W. Strothmann and Lawrence V. Ryan, "Hope for T. S. Eliot's 'Empty Men,'" *PMLA*, LXXIII (September, 1958), 426-432; Everett A. Gillis, Strothmann, and Ryan, "Hope for Eliot's Hollow Men?" *PMLA*, LXXV (December, 1960), 635-638; Leonard Unger, "*Ash Wednesday*," in *T. S. Eliot*, ed. Leonard Unger (New York, 1948), pp. 349-373; and Grover Smith, *T. S. Eliot's Poetry and Plays* (Chicago, 1960), pp. 137-138, *et passim*.
13. "As I am forgotten / And would be forgotten, so I would forget / Thus devoted, concentrated in purpose" (Part II) to the active purgation of the memory through hope in Chapter VI, or even to Book III, the active purgation of memory and will; "Under a juniper-tree the bones sang, scattered and shining" (Part II) to the bones and the marrow that rejoice and sing and are bathed in delight in Chapter XI; and the ascent of the stairway (Part III) to the ascent of the stairway in Chapter XII.
14. "Eliot of the Circle and John of the Cross," *Thought*, XXXIV (Spring, 1959), 127.
15. Quoted in Matthiessen, pp. 167-168.
16. *Ibid.*, p. 167.
17. *Poetry and Drama* (Cambridge, 1951), p. 38.
18. In his essay on Baudelaire he writes that "his business was not to practise Christianity, but—what was much more important for his time—to assert its *necessity*," *Selected Essays*, p. 374. See Cleanth Brooks' chapter on Eliot, "Discourse to the Gentiles," in *The Hidden God* (New Haven, 1963).
19. Jack Winter, "'Prufrockism' in *The Cocktail Party*," *MLQ*, XXII (June, 1961), 148.

CHAPTER V

1. See R. P. Blackmur, *Language as Gesture* (New York, 1952), pp. 301-316; Allen Tate, *Collected Essays* (Denver, 1959), pp. 225-237; Brom Weber, *Hart Crane* (New York, 1948); and Yvor Winters, *In Defense of Reason* (Denver, 1947), pp. 575-603. A major exception is Waldo Frank, Introduction to *The Collected Poems* (New

York, 1946). See H. D. Rowe, *Hart Crane: A Bibliography* (Denver, 1955).

2. Stanley K. Coffman, Jr., "Symbolism in *The Bridge*," *PMLA*, LXVI (March, 1951), 65-77; Lawrence S. Dembo, *Hart Crane's Sanskrit Charge* (Ithaca, 1960); Gordon K. Grigsby, "Hart Crane's Doubtful Vision," *CE*, XXIV (April, 1963), 518-523; Samuel Hazo, *Hart Crane* (New York, 1963); Jerome W. Kloucek, "The Framework of Hart Crane's *The Bridge*," *MidR* (Spring, 1960), 13-23; Sister M. Bernetta Quinn, *The Metamorphic Tradition in Modern Poetry* (New Brunswick, 1955), pp. 147-167; Vincent Quinn, *Hart Crane* (New York, 1963); Bernice Slote, "Transmutation in Crane's Imagery in *The Bridge*," *MLN*, LXXIII (January, 1958), 15-23, and "The Structure of Hart Crane's *The Bridge*," *UKCR*, XXIV (March, 1958), 225-238; and John R. Willingham, " 'Three Songs' of Hart Crane's *The Bridge*: A Reconsideration," *AL*, XXVII (March, 1955), 62-68, and "The Whitman Tradition in Recent American Literature" (Oklahoma, 1953).

3. Amos N. Wilder, *The Spiritual Aspects of the New Poetry* (New York, 1940), pp. 123-124.

4. For an appreciation of Hopkins, see the letter of 2/5/1928 to Samuel Loveman, p. 317. For an appreciation of Joyce's *Portrait*, see "Joyce and Ethics," *The Little Review* (July, 1918), reprinted in Weber, *Hart Crane*, pp. 402-403. For an early appreciation of Eliot, see the letter of 6/12/1922 to Allen Tate, p. 90.

5. Crane here seems to mean some kind of fulfillment with a loved one. There is in this letter a sentence which will shed light on the spiritual experience in *The Bridge*: "And I have been able to give freedom and life which was acknowledged in the ecstasy of walking hand in hand across the most beautiful bridge of the world, the cables enclosing us and pulling us upward in such a dance as I have never walked and never can walk with another," p. 181.

6. Introduction to *The Collected Poems*, pp. xiii-xiv.

7. *The Idea of the Holy*, trans. John W. Harvey, 2nd ed. (New York, 1960), p. 85, n. 1.

8. *The Modern Poets* (New York, 1960), p. 172.

9. Otto, p. 75.

10. Underhill, p. 196.

11. Dembo, pp. 66-81, *et passim*.

12. Coffman, "Symbolism in *The Bridge*," p. 69.

13. Both Philip Horton, *Hart Crane* (New York, 1937), pp. 115-116, and Dembo, p. 46, n. 1, refer to the similarity between Crane's imagery and Jacob Boehme's "visionary eye."

14. *Science and the Modern World* (New York, 1926), p. 3.

15. *Tertium Organum*, trans. Nicholas Bessaraboff and Claude Bragdon, 3rd American ed. (New York, 1945), pp. 230-231. Sum-

maries of this work and Frank's *Our America* are given in Weber, *Hart Crane*, pp. 150-174.

16. *Our America* (New York, 1919), p. 202.
17. *Virgin Spain* (New York, 1926), p. 166.
18. Underhill, p. 265.
19. For an excellent examination of the "Cape Hatteras" section, see Hyatt Howe Waggoner, *The Heel of Elohim* (Norman, 1950), pp. 177-184.
20. James E. Miller. Jr., in *A Critical Guide to "Leaves of Grass"* (Chicago, 1957), pp. 6-35, interprets "Song of Myself" according to Miss Underhill's fivehold division, with "some significant differences . . . central to the poet's meaning and intention," p. 7.
21. Wallace Fowlie, in *The Clown's Grail* (London, 1948), writes, "Throughout the various sections of *The Bridge*, images and flashes of phrases constantly recall the cult of the Virgin, her purity, her eternity, her pre-eminent rôle of mediatrix," p. 130.
22. Dembo, p. 65.
23. For a summary of this development, see Otto, pp. 109-110.
24. Frank, *Virgin Spain*, pp. 298-299.
25. Underhill, p. 51.
26. Slote, "Transmutation in Crane's Imagery in *The Bridge*," p. 22.
27. See the letters of 1/5/1923 to Gorham Munson, pp. 114-115; of 3/5/1926 to Gorham Munson, p. 236; of 9/7/1930 to Allen Tate, p. 355.
28. In a letter of 10/6/1921 to Gorham Munson, Crane lists Nietzsche among "mutual favorites" of himself and a friend, Willy Lescaze, pp. 66-67. See Dembo, pp. 12-23 and 26, n. 2.
29. Stace, pp. 333-340.
30. "The Framework of Hart Crane's *The Bridge*," pp. 22-23.

CHAPTER VI

1. William Barrett, *Irrational Man* (Garden City, 1958), p. 20.
2. *Christian Mysticism*, 8th ed. (London, 1948), pp. 117-119.
3. Emil Mersch, *The Theology of the Mystical Body*, trans. Cyril Vollert (St. Louis, 1958), pp. 482-483.
4. *Ibid.*, p. 485.
5. *The Idea of a Christian Society* (New York, 1940), p. 59.
6. *Ibid.*, p. 75.
7. Mersch, p. 313.
8. *The Idea of a Christian Society*, pp. 20-21.
9. Barrett, p. 21.

10. *Emergence from Chaos* (Boston, 1957), pp. 212-213.
11. Mersch, p. 591.
12. *Ibid.*, p. 484.
13. *T. S. Eliot's "Four Quartets"* (Copenhagen, 1958), p. 99.
14. Holroyd, p. 211.
15. Mersch, p. 241.

A Selected Bibliography

Except for those articles which are given their original journal appearances in my notes, articles which first appeared in collections of essays on the four authors and articles which have since appeared in such collections are not given separate entries.

Alighieri, Dante. *Commedia.* Temple Classics edition. 3 vols. London: J. M. Dent and Sons, 1958, 1956, 1958.

———. *La Vita Nuova.* Temple Classics edition. London: J. M. Dent, 1906.

Allison, Alexander W. "Hopkins' 'I wake and feel the fell of dark,'" *Expl,* XVII (May, 1959), Item 54.

Anderson C. G. "The Sacrificial Butter," *Accent,* XII (Winter, 1952), 3-13.

Anthony, Mother Mary, S. H. C. J. "Verbal Pattern in 'Burnt Norton I,'" *Criticism,* II (Winter, 1960), 81-89.

Arrowsmith, William. *"The Cocktail Party," Hudson Review,* III (Autumn, 1950), 411-430.

———. "Transfiguration in Eliot and Euripides," *SR,* LXIII (Summer, 1955), 421-442.

Augustine, Saint. *Confessions.* Translated by John K. Ryan. Garden City, New York: Image Books, 1960.

Baker, James R. "James Joyce: Affirmation after Exile," *MLQ,* XVIII (December, 1957), 275-281.

———. "James Joyce: Esthetic Freedom and Dramatic Art," *WHR,* V (Winter, 1950-1951), 29-40.

Barrett, William. *Irrational Man.* Garden City, New York: Doubleday, 1958.

Barth, J. Robert, S. J. "T. S. Eliot's Image of Man: A Thematic Study of his Drama," *Ren,* XIV (Spring, 1962), 126-138.

Battenhouse, Roy W. "Eliot's 'The Family Reunion' as Christian Prophecy," *Christendom,* X (Summer, 1945), 307-321.

Beebe, Maurice. "James Joyce and Giordano Bruno: A Possible Source for 'Dedalus,'" *JJR,* I (December, 1957), 41-45.

————. "James Joyce: Barnacle Goose and Lapwing," *PMLA,* LXXI (June, 1956), 302-320.

Bender, Todd K. "Hopkins' 'God's Grandeur,'" *Expl,* XXI (March, 1963), Item 55.

Benziger, James. *Images of Eternity.* Carbondale: Southern Illinois University Press, 1962.

Bergsten, Staffan. "Illusive Allusions: Some Reflections on the Critical Approach to the Poetry of T. S. Eliot," *OL,* XIV (1959), 9-18.

————. *Time and Eternity.* Stockholm: Svenska Bokförlaget, 1960.

Bernad, Miguel A., S. J. "Hopkins' 'Pied Beauty': A Note on Its Ignatian Inspiration," *EIC,* XII (April, 1962), 217-220.

Bernhardt-Kabisch, E. "Joyce's *A Portrait of the Artist as a Young Man,*" *Expl,* XVIII (January, 1960), Item 24.

Bischoff, D. A., S. J. "The Manuscripts of Gerard Manley Hopkins," *Thought,* XXVI (Winter, 1951), 551-580.

Blackmur, R. P. *Language as Gesture.* New York: Harcourt, Brace, 1952.

Bland, D. S. "T. S. Eliot's Case-Book," *MLN,* LXXV (January, 1960), 23-26.

————. "The Tragic Hero in Modern Literature," *Cambridge Journal,* III (January, 1950), 214-223.

Blissett, William. "The Argument of T. S. Eliot's *Four Quartets,*" *UTQ,* XV (January, 1946), 115-126.

Boardman, Gwenn R. "*Ash Wednesday*: Eliot's Lenten Mass Sequence," *Ren,* XV (Fall, 1962), 28-36.

Bodelsen, C. A. *T. S. Eliot's "Four Quartets."* Copenhagen: Rosenkilde and Bagger, 1958.

Bodkin, Maud. *Archetypal Patterns in Poetry.* London: Oxford University Press, 1934.

——. *The Quest for Salvation in an Ancient and a Modern Play.* London: Oxford University Press, 1941.

——. *Studies of Type-Images in Poetry, Religion, and Philosophy.* London: Oxford University Press, 1951.

Booth, Wayne C. *The Rhetoric of Fiction.* Chicago: University of Chicago Press, 1961.

Boyle, Robert, S. J. *Metaphor in Hopkins.* Chapel Hill: University of North Carolina Press, 1961.

Bradbrook, M. C. *T. S. Eliot.* Writers and Their Work. No. 8. London: Longmans, Green, 1958.

Bradbury, John M. "*Four Quartets*: The Structural Symbolism," SR, LIX (Spring, 1951), 254-270.

Bradford, Curtis. "Footnotes to *East Coker*: A Reading," SR, LII (Winter, 1944), 169-175.

Bremond, Henri. *Prayer and Poetry.* Translated by Algar Thorold. London: Burns Oates and Washbourne, 1927.

Brett, R. L. *Reason and Imagination.* London: Oxford University Press, 1960.

Brooks, Cleanth. *The Hidden God.* New Haven: Yale University Press, 1963.

Brotman, D. Bosley. "T. S. Eliot: 'The Music of Ideas,'" UTQ, XVIII (October, 1948), 20-29.

Budgen, Frank. *James Joyce and the Making of "Ulysses."* 2nd ed. London: Grayson and Grayson, 1937.

Butler, Cuthbert, O. S. B. *Western Mysticism.* New York: E. P. Dutton, 1924.

Byrne, J. F. *Silent Years.* New York: Farrar, Straus and Cudahy, 1953.

Cargill, Oscar. *Intellectual America.* New York: Macmillan, 1941.

Cattaui, Georges. *Trois Poëtes.* Paris: Egloff, 1947.

Church, Margaret. "Eliot's 'Journey of the Magi,'" *Expl*, XVIII (June, 1960), Item 55.

Cleophas, Sister M., R. S. M. "*Ash Wednesday:* The *Purgatorio* in a Modern Mode," *CL*, XI (Fall, 1959), 329-339.

——. "Notes on Levels of Meaning in 'Four Quartets,'" *Ren*, II (Spring, 1950), 102-116.

Clubb, Merrel D., Jr. "The Heraclitean Element in Eliot's *Four Quartets*," *PQ*, XL (January, 1961), 19-33.

Coanda, Richard. "Hopkins and Donne: 'Mystic' and Metaphysical," *Ren*, IX (Summer, 1957), 180-187.

Coffman, Stanley K., Jr. "Symbolism in *The Bridge*," *PMLA*, LXVI (March, 1951), 65-77.

Colby, Robert A. "Orpheus in the Counting House: *The Confidential Clerk*," *PMLA*, LXXII (September, 1957), 791-802.

——. "The Three Worlds of *The Cocktail Party*: The Wit of T. S. Eliot," *UTQ*, XXIV (October, 1954), 56-69.

Colum, Mary and Padraic. *Our Friend James Joyce*. Garden City, New York: Doubleday, 1958.

Cornwell, Ethel F. *The "Still Point."* New Brunswick: Rutgers University Press, 1962.

Crane, Hart. *The Collected Poems of Hart Crane*, ed. Waldo Frank. Black and Gold edition. New York: Liveright, 1946.

——. *The Letters of Hart Crane: 1916-1932*, ed. Brom Weber. New York: Hermitage House, 1952.

Daiches, David. "James Joyce: The Artist as Exile," in *Forms of Modern Fiction*, ed. William Van O'Connor. Minneapolis: University of Minnesota Press, 1948.

——. *The Novel and the Modern World*. Rev. ed. Chicago: University of Chicago Press, 1960.

Dedalus on Crete, ed. Joseph Feehan. Los Angeles: Immaculate Heart College, 1956.

de Guibert, Joseph, S. J. *The Theology of the Spiritual Life*. Translated by Paul Barrett. New York: Sheed and Ward, 1953.

Dembo, Lawrence S. *Hart Crane's Sanskrit Charge*. Ithaca: Cornell University Press, 1960.

Digges, Sister M. Laurentia, C. S. J. "Gerard Manley Hopkins's Sonnets of Desolation: An Analysis of Meaning." Unpublished doctoral dissertation, Catholic University, 1951.

Dobrée, Bonamy. "The Confidential Clerk." *SR*, LXII (January-March, 1954), 117-131.

Donoghue, Denis. "The Bird as Symbol," *Studies*, XLIV (Autumn, 1955), 291-299.

Dougherty, Charles T. "Joyce and Ruskin," *NQ*, CXCVIII (February, 1953), 76-77.

Downes, David A. *Gerard Manley Hopkins: A Study of His Ignatian Spirit*. New York: Bookman Associates, 1959.

Doyle, Francis G., S. J. "A Note on Hopkins' 'Windhover,' " *Studies*, XLV (Spring, 1956), 88-91.

Drew, Arnold P. "Hints and Guesses in *Four Quartets*," *UKCR*, XX (Spring, 1954), 171-175.

Drew, Elizabeth. *T. S. Eliot: The Design of His Poetry*. New York: Charles Scribner's Sons, 1949.

Dundes, Alan. "Re: Joyce—No In at the Womb," *MFS*, VIII (Summer, 1962), 137-147.

Edel, Leon. *The Psychological Novel: 1900-1950*. Philadelphia: J. B. Lippincott, 1955.

Eleanor, Mother Mary. "Eliot's Magi," *Ren*, X (Autumn, 1957), 26-31.

Eliot, T. S. *After Strange Gods: A Primer of Modern Heresy*. New York: Harcourt, Brace, 1934.

———. *The Complete Poems and Plays: 1909-1950*. New York: Harcourt, Brace, 1952.

———. *The Confidential Clerk*. New York: Harcourt, Brace, 1954.

———. *The Elder Statesman*. New York: Farrar, Straus and Cudahy, 1959.

Eliot, T. S. *The Idea of a Christian Society.* New York: Harcourt, Brace, 1940.

———. *Notes towards the Definition of Culture.* New York: Harcourt, Brace, 1949.

———. *Poetry and Drama.* Cambridge: Harvard University Press, 1951.

———. *Selected Essays.* New ed. New York: Harcourt, Brace, 1950.

T. S. Eliot: A Collection of Critical Essays, ed. Hugh Kenner. Englewood Cliffs: Prentice-Hall, 1962.

T. S. Eliot: A Selected Critique, ed. Leonard Unger. New York: Rinehart, 1948.

T. S. Eliot: A Study of His Writings by Several Hands, ed. B. Rajan. London: Dennis Dobson, 1947.

T. S. Eliot: A Symposium, ed. Richard March and Tambimuttu. London: PL Editions Poetry, 1948.

T. S. Eliot: A Symposium for His Seventieth Birthday, ed. Neville Braybrooke. New York: Farrar, Straus and Cudahy, 1958.

Ellmann, Richard. *James Joyce.* New York: Oxford University Press, 1959.

Fairchild, Hoxie N. *Religious Trends in English Poetry.* 5 vols. New York: Columbia University Press, 1939-1962.

Fergusson, Francis. *The Idea of a Theater.* Princeton: Princeton University Press, 1949.

———. "Three Allegorists: Brecht, Wilder and Eliot," *SR,* LXIV (Autumn, 1956), 544-573.

Fleming, Rudd. "Dramatic Involution: Tate, Husserl, and Joyce," *SR,* LX (Summer, 1952), 445-464.

———. *"The Elder Statesman* and Eliot's 'Programme for the Métier of Poetry,' " *WSCL,* II (Winter, 1961), 54-64.

———. *"Quidditas* in the Tragi-Comedy of Joyce," *UKCR,* XV (Summer, 1949), 288-296.

Foster, Genevieve W. "The Archetypal Imagery of T. S. Eliot," *PMLA,* LX (June, 1945), 567-585.

Fowlie, Wallace. *The Clown's Grail*. London: Dennis Dobson, 1948.

Frank, Waldo. *Our America*. New York: Boni and Liveright, 1919.

———. *Virgin Spain*. New York: Boni and Liveright, 1926.

Friedman, Melvin J. *Stream of Consciousness*. New Haven: Yale University Press, 1956.

Frierson, William C. *The English Novel in Transition*. Norman: University of Oklahoma Press, 1942.

Fussell, B. H. "Structural Methods in *Four Quartets*," *ELH*, XXII (September, 1955), 212-241.

Gallup, Donald. *T. S. Eliot: A Bibliography*. London: Faber and Faber, 1952.

Gardner, Helen. *The Art of T. S. Eliot*. London: Cresset, 1961.

———, editor. *John Donne: The Divine Poems*. London: Oxford University Press, 1952.

———, editor with G. M. Story. *The Sonnets of William Alabaster*. London: Oxford University Press, 1959.

Gardner, W. H. *Gerard Manley Hopkins (1844-1889): A Study of Poetic Idiosyncrasy in Relation to Poetic Tradition*. 2nd ed., rev. 2 vols. London: Oxford University Press, 1961.

Garrigou-Lagrange, R., O. P. *The Three Ages of the Interior Life*. Translated by Sister M. Timothea Doyle. 2 vols. St. Louis: B. Herder, 1960.

Gaskell, Ronald. "'The Family Reunion,'" *EIC*, XII (July, 1962), 292-301.

Gavin, Sister Rosemarie Julie, S. N. D. de N. "Hopkins' 'The Candle Indoors,'" *Expl*, XX (February, 1962), Item 50.

George, A. G. *T. S. Eliot: His Mind and Art*. London: Asia Publishing House, 1962.

Gerard, Sister Mary, S. N. D. de N. "Eliot of the Circle and John of the Cross," *Thought*, XXXIV (Spring, 1959), 107-127.

Gillis, Everett A., Strothmann, and Ryan. "Hope for Eliot's Hollow Men?" *PMLA*, LXXV (December, 1960), 635-638.

Glicksberg, Charles I. "The Journey that Must Be Taken: Spiritual Quest in T. S. Eliot's Plays," *SWR*, XL (Summer, 1955), 203-210.

Goldberg, S. L. *The Classical Temper.* New York: Barnes and Noble, 1961.

Golding, Louis. *James Joyce.* London: Thornton Butterworth, 1933.

Goodier, Alban, S. J. *An Introduction to the Study of Ascetical and Mystical Theology.* Milwaukee: Bruce, 1957.

Gordon, Caroline. *How to Read a Novel.* New York: Viking, 1957.

————. "Some Readings and Misreadings," *SR*, LXI (July-September, 1953), 384-407.

Gorman, Herbert. *James Joyce.* New York: Rinehart, 1948.

Greiner, Francis J., S. M. "Hopkins' 'The Habit of Perfection,'" *Expl*, XXI (November, 1962), Item 19.

Grigsby, Gordon K. "Hart Crane's Doubtful Vision," *CE*, XXIV (April, 1963), 518-523.

Grigson, Geoffrey. *Gerard Manley Hopkins.* Writers and Their Work. No. 59. London: Longmans, Green, 1958.

Gross, Harvey Seymour. "The Contrived Corridor: A Study in Modern Poetry and the Meaning of History." Unpublished doctoral dissertation, University of Michigan, 1955.

Hamalian, Leo. "Mr. Eliot's Saturday Evening Service," *Accent*, X (Autumn, 1950), 195-206.

————. "Wishwood Revisited," *Ren*, XII (Summer, 1960), 167-173.

Hanzo, Thomas. "Eliot and Kierkegaard: 'The Meaning of Happening' in *The Cocktail Party*," *MD*, III (May, 1960), 52-59.

Harding, D. W. "Progression of Theme in Eliot's Modern Plays," *KR*, XVIII (Summer, 1956), 337-360.

Hardy, John Edward. "An Antic Disposition," *SR*, LXV (Winter, 1957), 50-60.

Hart, Sister M. Adorita, B. V. M. "The Christocentric Theme in Gerard Manley Hopkins's 'The Wreck of the Deutschland.'" Unpublished doctoral dissertation, Catholic University, 1952.

Hartman, Geoffrey H. *The Unmediated Vision*. New Haven: Yale University Press, 1954.

Hazo, Samuel. *Hart Crane: An Introduction and Interpretation*. New York: Barnes and Noble, 1963.

Heiler, Friedrich. *Prayer*. Translated and ed. by Samuel McComb. London: Oxford University Press, 1932.

Heilman, Robert B. "*Alcestis* and *The Cocktail Party*," *CL*, V (Spring, 1953), 105-116.

Heuser, Alan. *The Shaping Vision of Gerard Manley Hopkins*. London: Oxford University Press, 1958.

Hill, Archibald A. "An Analysis of *The Windhover*: An Experiment in Structural Method," *PMLA*, LX (December, 1955), 968-978.

Hoffman, Frederick J. *The Twenties*. New York: Viking, 1955.

Holroyd, Stuart. *Emergence from Chaos*. Boston: Houghton Mifflin, 1957.

Honig, Edwin. "Hobgoblin or Apollo," *KR*, X (Autumn, 1948), 664-681.

Hopkins, Gerard Manley. *The Journals and Papers of Gerard Manley Hopkins*, ed. Humphry House and Graham Storey. London: Oxford University Press, 1959.

——. *The Letters of Gerard Manley Hopkins to Robert Bridges*, ed. C. C. Abbott. Rev. ed. London: Oxford University Press, 1955.

——. *Poems of Gerard Manley Hopkins*. 3rd ed., enl. and ed. W. H. Gardner, 1948. 5th impression, rev., with additional poems, 1956. London: Oxford University Press, 1960.

——. *The Sermons and Devotional Writings of Gerard*

Manley Hopkins, ed. Christopher Devlin, S. J. London: Oxford University Press, 1959.

Gerard Manley Hopkins, ed. the Kenyon Critics. Norfolk: New Directions, 1945.

Horton, Philip. *Hart Crane: The Life of an American Poet.* New York: W. W. Norton, 1937.

Humiliata, Sister Mary. "Hopkins and the Prometheus Myth," *PMLA,* LXX (March, 1955), 58-68.

Humphrey, Robert. *Stream of Consciousness in the Modern Novel.* Berkeley: University of California Press, 1954.

Ignatius Loyola, Saint. *Spiritual Exercises.* Translated, with a trans. of the *Directorium in Exercitia,* by W. H. Longridge. 5th ed. London: A. R. Mowbray, 1955.

Immortal Diamond: Studies in Gerard Manley Hopkins, ed. Norman Weyand, S. J. New York: Sheed and Ward, 1949.

Inge, William Ralph. *Christian Mysticism.* 8th ed. London: Methuen, 1948.

Jedynak, Stanley Louis. "Epiphany and Dantean Correspondence in Joyce's *Dubliners:* A Study in Structure." Unpublished doctoral dissertation, Syracuse University, 1962.

John of the Cross, Saint. *The Complete Works.* Translated and ed. by E. Allison Peers. 3 vols. London: Burns Oates and Washbourne, 1934.

Johnson, W. Stacey. "The Imagery of Gerard Manley Hopkins: Fire, Light, and the Incarnation," *VN,* No. 16 (Fall, 1959), 18-23.

Jones, David E. *The Plays of T. S. Eliot.* London: Routledge and Kegan Paul, 1962.

Jones, William Powell. *James Joyce and the Common Reader.* Norman: University of Oklahoma Press, 1955.

Joyce, James. *The Critical Writings of James Joyce,* ed. Ellsworth Mason and Richard Ellmann. New York: Viking, 1959.

——. *Epiphanies of James Joyce,* ed. O. A. Silverman. Buffalo: Lockwood Memorial Library, 1956.

———. "The First Version of Joyce's 'Portrait,'" ed. Richard M. Kain and Robert E. Scholes, *YR*, XLIX (Spring, 1960), 355-370.

———. *A Portrait of the Artist as a Young Man*. New ed., 1924. Illustrated ed., 1956. London: Jonathan Cape, 1960.

———. *Stephen Hero*, ed. Theodore Spencer, incorporating the additional manuscript pages, ed. John J. Slocum and Herbert Cahoon. New York: New Directions, 1955.

———. *Ulysses*. New York: Random House, 1946.

A James Joyce Miscellany, ed. Marvin Magalaner. New York: The James Joyce Society, 1957.

———. 2nd Ser., ed. Marvin Magalaner. Carbondale: Southern Illinois University Press, 1959.

———. 3rd Ser., ed. Marvin Magalaner. Carbondale: Southern Illinois University Press, 1962.

James Joyce: Two Decades of Criticism, ed. Seon Givens. New York: Vanguard, 1948.

Joyce's "Portrait": Criticisms and Critiques, ed. Thomas E. Connolly. New York: Appleton-Century-Crofts, 1962.

Joyce, Stanislaus. *My Brother's Keeper*, ed. Richard Ellmann. New York: Viking, 1958.

Kaplan, Robert B., and Wall, Richard J. "Eliot's 'Journey of the Magi,'" *Expl*, XIX (November, 1960), Item 8.

Kaye, Julian B. "Who Is Betty Byrne?" *MLN*, LXXI (February, 1956), 93-95.

Kelly, Hugh, S. J. "'The Windhover'—and Christ," *Studies*, XLV (Summer, 1956), 188-193.

Kenner, Hugh. *Dublin's Joyce*. Bloomington: Indiana University Press, 1956.

———. *The Invisible Poet*. New York: McDowell, Obolensky, 1959.

Kissane, James. "Classical Echoes in Hopkins' 'Heaven-Haven,'" *MLN*, LXXIII (November, 1958), 491-492.

Kligerman, Jack. "An Interpretation of T. S. Eliot's 'East Coker,'" *ArQ*, XVIII (Summer, 1962), 101-112.

Kline, Peter. "The Spiritual Center in Eliot's Plays," *KR*, XXI (Summer, 1959), 457-472.

Kloucek, Jerome W. "The Framework of Hart Crane's *The Bridge*," *MidR* (Spring, 1960), 13-23.

Knieger, Bernard. "The Dramatic Achievement of T. S. Eliot," *MD*, III (February, 1961), 387-392.

Knox, George A. "Quest for the Word in Eliot's *Four Quartets*," *ELH*, XVIII (December, 1951), 310-321.

Kumar, Shiv K. *Bergson and the Stream of Consciousness Novel*. New York: New York University Press, 1963.

Lahey, G. F., S. J. *Gerard Manley Hopkins*. London: Oxford University Press, 1930.

Lawlor, John. "The Formal Achievement of 'The Cocktail Party,'" *VQR*, XXX (Spring, 1954), 431-451.

Leavis, F. R. *Education and the University*. London: Chatto and Windus, 1943.

————. *New Bearings in English Poetry*. London: Chatto and Windus, 1932.

Levin, Harry. *James Joyce: A Critical Introduction*. Rev. and aug. ed. Norfolk: New Directions, 1960.

Lewis, Arthur O., Jr. "Eliot's *Four Quartets*: Burnt Norton IV," *Expl*, VIII (November, 1949), Item 9.

Lewis, Wyndham. *Time and Western Man*. New York: Harcourt, Brace, 1928.

Licht, Merete. "'What Is the Meaning of Happening?'" *OL*, XIV (1959), 19-32.

Lind, Ilse Dusoir. "*The Way of All Flesh* and *A Portrait of the Artist as a Young Man*: A Comparison," *VN*, No. 9 (Spring, 1956), 7-10.

Litz, Walton. "Early Vestiges of Joyce's *Ulysses*," *PMLA*, LXXI (March, 1956), 51-60.

Litzinger, Boyd. "The Genesis of Hopkins' 'Heaven-Haven,'" *VN*, No. 17 (Spring, 1960), 31-33.

————. "Hopkins' 'The Habit of Perfection,'" *Expl*, XVI (October, 1957), Item 1.

Lucy, Seán. *T. S. Eliot and the Idea of Tradition*. London: Cohen and West, 1960.

MacCallum, Reid. *Imitation and Design and Other Essays*, ed. William Blissett. Toronto: University of Toronto Press, 1953.

————. *Time Lost and Regained*. Toronto: The Sisters of the Church, 1949 (mimeo).

Madhusudan, Reddy V. "The Concept of Time in T. S. Eliot's *Four Quartets*," *OJES*, No. 1 (1961), 31-38.

Magalaner, Marvin. "James Mangan and Joyce's Dedalus Family," *PQ*, XXXI (October, 1952), 363-371.

Magalaner, Marvin and Kain, Richard M. *Joyce: The Man, the Work, the Reputation*. New York: New York University Press, 1956.

Martin, Philip M. *Mastery and Mercy*. London: Oxford University Press, 1957.

Martz, Louis L. *The Poetry of Meditation*. New Haven: Yale University Press, 1954.

Mason, Ellsworth. "Joyce's Categories," *SR*, LXI (Summer, 1953), 427-432.

Masters, Charlie. "Some Observations on 'Burnt Norton,'" *American Prefaces*, VI (Winter, 1941), 99-112; (Spring, 1941), 212-231.

Mathewson, George. "The Search for Coherence: T. S. Eliot and the Christian Tradition in English Poetry." Unpublished doctoral dissertation, Princeton University, 1961.

Matthiessen, F. O. *The Achievement of T. S. Eliot*. With a chapter on Eliot's later work by C. L. Barber. 3rd ed., rev. and enl. New York: Oxford University Press, 1958.

Maxwell, D. E. S. *The Poetry of T. S. Eliot*. London: Routledge and Kegan Paul, 1958.

McCarthy, Harold E. "T. S. Eliot and Buddhism," *PE&W*, II (April, 1952), 31-55.

McCrystal, Irene. "An Explication of Part V of T. S. Eliot's

Ash Wednesday." Unpublished master's thesis, Catholic University, 1953.

McDonnell, Thomas P. "Hopkins as a Sacramental Poet: A Reply to Yvor Winters," *Ren,* XIV (Autumn, 1961), 25-33.

McLaughlin, John J. "A Daring Metaphysic: *The Cocktail Party,"* *Ren,* III (Autumn, 1950), 15-28.

McNamee, M. B., S. J. "Mastery and Mercy in *The Wreck of the Deutschland,"* *CE,* XXIII (January, 1962), 267-276.

Mercer, Caroline G. "Stephen Dedalus's Vision and Synge's Peasant Girls," *NQ,* VII (December, 1960), 473-474.

Mercier, Vivian. *The Irish Comic Tradition.* Oxford: Clarendon Press, 1962.

Mersch, Emil, S. J. *The Theology of the Mystical Body.* Translated by Cyril Vollert. St. Louis: B. Herder, 1958.

Meyerhoff, Hans. *Time in Literature.* Berkeley: University of California Press, 1955.

Miller, James E., Jr. *A Critical Guide to "Leaves of Grass."* Chicago: University of Chicago Press, 1957.

Miller, James E., Jr., Shapiro, Karl, and Slote, Bernice. *Start with the Sun.* Lincoln: University of Nebraska Press, 1960.

Miller, J. Hillis. *The Disappearance of God.* Cambridge: Harvard University Press, 1963.

Moore, Dom Sebastian. "East Coker: The Place and the Poem," in *Focus Two,* ed. B. Rajan and A. Pearse. London: Dennis Dobson, 1946.

Morin, Edward. "Joyce as Thomist," *Ren,* IX (Spring, 1957), 127-131.

Morris, David. *The Poetry of Gerard Manley Hopkins and T. S. Eliot in the Light of the Donne Tradition.* Bern: A. Francke, 1953.

Morse, J. Mitchell. "The Artist as Savior," *MFS,* V (Summer, 1959), 103-107.

———. *The Sympathetic Alien.* New York: New York University Press, 1959.

Moseley, Virginia D. "James Joyce's 'Grave of Boyhood,'" *Ren*, XIII (Autumn, 1960), 10-20.

Musgrove, Stanley. *T. S. Eliot and Walt Whitman*. Wellington: New Zealand University Press, 1952.

New Testament. Translated from the original Greek by James A. Kleist, S. J., and Joseph L. Lilly, C. M. Milwaukee: Bruce, 1956.

Noon, William T., S. J. *"Four Quartets: Contemplatio ad Amorem,"* *Ren*, VII (Autumn, 1954), 3-10.

———. "James Joyce: Unfacts, Fiction, and Facts," *PMLA*, LXXVI (June, 1961), 254-276.

———. *Joyce and Aquinas*. New Haven: Yale University Press, 1957.

———. "Modern Literature and the Sense of Time," *Thought*, XXXIII (Winter, 1958-1959), 571-603.

Nott, Kathleen. *The Emperor's Clothes*. London: William Heinemann, 1953.

O'Connor, Frank. *The Mirror in the Roadway*. New York: Alfred A. Knopf, 1956.

Oden, Thomas C. "The Christology of T. S. Eliot: A Study of the Kerygma in 'Burnt Norton,'" *Encounter*, XXI (Winter, 1960), 93-101.

On the "Four Quartets" of T. S. Eliot. With a Foreword by Roy Campbell. London: V. Stuart, 1953.

Onesta, P. A., "The Self in Hopkins," *ESA*, IV (September, 1961), 174-181.

Otto, Rudolf. *The Idea of the Holy*. Translated by John W. Harvey. 2nd ed. London: Oxford University Press, 1950.

Ouspensky, P. D. *Tertium Organum*. Translated by Nicholas Bessaraboff and Claude Bragdon. 3rd American ed., auth. and rev. New York: Alfred A. Knopf, 1945.

Palmer, Richard E. "Existentialism in T. S. Eliot's *The Family Reunion*," *MD*, V (September, 1962), 174-186.

Parente, Pascal P. *The Ascetical Life*. Rev. ed. St. Louis: B. Herder, 1955.

Parente, Pascal P. *The Mystical Life*. St. Louis: B. Herder, 1956.

Pearce, Donald R. " 'My Dead King!': The Dinner Quarrel in Joyce's 'Portrait of the Artist,' " *MLN*, LXVI (April, 1951), 249-251.

Pearce, Roy Harvey. *The Continuity of American Poetry*. Princeton: Princeton University Press, 1961.

Perkins, David. "Rose Garden to Midwinter Spring: Achieved Faith in the *Four Quartets*," *MLQ*, XXIII (March, 1962), 41-45.

Peter, John. " 'The Family Reunion,' " *Scrutiny*, XVI (September, 1949), 219-230.

Peters, W. A. M., S. J. *Gerard Manley Hopkins: A Critical Essay towards the Understanding of his Poetry*. London: Oxford University Press, 1948.

Phare, Elsie Elizabeth. *The Poetry of Gerard Manley Hopkins*. Cambridge, England: The University Press, 1933.

Pick, John. *Gerard Manley Hopkins: Priest and Poet*. London: Oxford University Press, 1942.

The Portable Nietzsche. Translated and ed. by Walter Kaufmann. New York: Viking, 1954.

Portalié, Eugène, S. J. *A Guide to the Thought of St. Augustine*. Translated by Ralph J. Bastian. Chicago: Henry Regnery, 1960.

Poss, S. H. "A Portrait of the Artist as Beginner," *UKCR*, XXVI (March, 1960), 189-196.

Poulain, August, S. J. *The Graces of Interior Prayer*. Translated from the 6th ed. by Leonora L. Yorke Smith and corrected to accord with the 10th French ed. St. Louis: B. Herder, 1950.

Pourrat, Pierre, S. S. *Christian Spirituality*. Translated by Donald Attwater, S. P. Jacques, and W. H. Mitchell. 4 vols. Westminster: Newman, 1953-1955.

Praz, Mario. *The Flaming Heart*. Garden City, New York: Doubleday, 1958.

Prescott, Joseph. "James Joyce: A Study in Words," *PMLA*, LIV (March, 1939), 304-315.

———. "James Joyce's Epiphanies," *MLN*, LXIV (May, 1949), 346.

Preston, Raymond. *"Four Quartets" Rehearsed*. New York: Sheed and Ward, 1946.

Quinn, Sister M. Bernetta. *The Metamorphic Tradition in Modern Poetry*. New Brunswick: Rutgers University Press, 1955.

Quinn, Vincent. *Hart Crane*. New York: Twayne, 1963.

Redford, Grant H. "The Role of Structure in Joyce's 'Portrait,'" *MFS*, IV (Spring, 1958), 21-30.

Reinsberg, Mark. "A Footnote to *Four Quartets*," *AL*, XXI (November, 1949), 343-344.

Robbins, Rossell Hope. *The T. S. Eliot Myth*. New York: Henry Schuman, 1951.

Roberts, John H. "James Joyce: From Religion to Art," *New Humanist*, VII (May-June, 1934), 7-13.

Rosenthal, M. L. *The Modern Poets*. New York: Oxford University Press, 1960.

Rowe, H. D. *Hart Crane: A Bibliography*. Denver: Alan Swallow, 1955.

Rudd, Margaret. *Divided Image*. London: Routledge and Kegan Paul, 1953.

Ruggles, Eleanor. *Gerard Manley Hopkins: A Life*. New York: W. W. Norton, 1944.

Ryf, Robert S. *A New Approach to Joyce*. Berkeley: University of California Press, 1962.

Savage, D. S. *The Withered Branch*. London: Eyre and Spottiswoode, 1950.

Schaar, Claes. "Palimpsest Technique in 'Little Gidding': The Second Movement and the 'Inferno,' XV," *OL*, XIV (1959), 33-37.

Schenk, Willy. "The Experience and the Meaning," *Humanitas*, I (June, 1947), 23-27.

Scheve, Brother Adelbert, F. S. C. "Hopkins' 'The Wreck of the Deutschland,' Stanza 33, " *Expl*, XVII (June, 1959), Item 60.

Schneider, Elisabeth. "Hopkins' 'The Windhover,'" *Expl*, XVIII (January, 1960), Item 22.

Schoder, Raymond V., S. J. " 'Spelt from Sibyl's Leaves,'" *Thought*, XIX (December, 1944), 633-648.

Scholes, Robert. "Joyce and the Epiphany: The Key to the Labyrinth?" *SR*, LXXII (Winter, 1964), 65-77.

Schorer, Mark. "Technique as Discovery," in *Forms of Modern Fiction*, ed. William Van O'Connor. Minneapolis: University of Minnesota Press, 1948.

Schwartz, Edward. "Eliot's *Cocktail Party* and the New Humanism," *PQ*, XXXII (January, 1953), 58-68.

———. "Joyce's *Portrait*," *Expl*, XI (February, 1953), Item 27.

Seward, Barbara. "The Artist and the Rose," *UTQ*, XXVI (January, 1957), 180-190.

———. *The Symbolic Rose*. New York: Columbia University Press, 1960.

Shapiro, Leo. "The Medievalism of T. S. Eliot," *Poetry*, LVI (July, 1940), 202-213.

Sharpe, Garold. "The Philosophy of James Joyce," *MFS*, IX (Summer, 1963), 120-126.

Shuman, R. Baird. "Buddhistic Overtones in Eliot's *The Cocktail Party*," *MLN*, LXXII (June, 1957), 426-427.

———. "Eliot's *The Cocktail Party*," *Expl*, XVII (April, 1959), Item 46.

Simister, O. E. "The *Four Quartets*—And Other Observations," *AWR*, X, No. 26, 39-45.

Slote, Bernice. "The Structure of Hart Crane's *The Bridge*," *UKCR*, XXIV (March, 1958), 225-238.

———. "Transmutation in Crane's Imagery in *The Bridge*," *MLN*, LXXIII (January, 1958), 15-23.

Smidt, Kristian. *James Joyce and the Cultic Use of Fiction.* Oslo: Akademisk Forlag, 1955.

———. *Poetry and Belief in the Work of T. S. Eliot.* Rev. ed. New York: Humanities, 1961.

———. "Point of View in Eliot's Poetry," *OL,* XIV (1959), 38-53.

Smith, Carol H. *T. S. Eliot's Dramatic Theory and Practice.* Princeton: Princeton University Press, 1963.

Smith, Grover. *T. S. Eliot's Poetry and Plays.* Chicago: University of Chicago Press, 1960.

———. "The Ghosts in T. S. Eliot's 'The Elder Statesman,'" *NQ,* VII (June, 1960), 233-235.

Spencer, Theodore. "On 'Murder in the Cathedral,'" *Harvard Advocate,* CXXV (December, 1938), 21-22.

Spender, Stephen. *The Creative Element.* London: H. Hamilton, 1953.

———. *The Destructive Element.* London: Jonathan Cape, 1935.

Stace, W. T. *Mysticism and Philosophy.* New York: J. B. Lippincott, 1960.

Stamm, Rudolf. "The Orestes Theme in Three Plays by Eugene O'Neill, T. S. Eliot, and Jean-Paul Sartre," *ES,* XXX (October, 1949), 244-255.

Stanford, Derek. "T. S. Eliot's New Play," *QQ,* LXV (Winter, 1959), 682-689.

Stanford, W. B. "The Mysticism That Pleased Him," *Envoy,* V (Special Number, April, 1951), 62-69.

———. *The Ulysses Theme.* Oxford: Blackwell, 1954.

Stelzmann, Rainulf A. "The Theology of T. S. Eliot's Dramas," *XUS,* I (April, 1961), 7-17.

Stephenson, A. A., S. J. "G. M. Hopkins and John Donne," *Downside Review,* LXXVII (Summer-Autumn, 1959), 300-320.

Stephenson, E. M. *T. S. Eliot and the Lay Reader.* London: Fortune, 1944.

Stern, Richard G. "Proust and Joyce Underway: Jean Santeuil and Stephen Hero," *KR*, XVIII (Summer, 1956), 486-496.

Stewart, J. I. M. *James Joyce*. Writers and Their Work. No. 91. London: Longmans, Green, 1960.

Strong, L. A. G. *The Sacred River*. New York: Pellegrini and Cudahy, 1951.

Strothmann, Friedrich W. and Ryan, Lawrence V. "Hope for T. S. Eliot's 'Empty Men,'" *PMLA*, LXXIII (September, 1958), 426-432.

Sullivan, Kevin. *Joyce among the Jesuits*. New York: Columbia University Press, 1958.

Sypher, Wylie. "Portrait of the Artist as John Keats," *VQR*, XXV (Summer, 1949), 420-428.

Tate, Allen. *Collected Essays*. Denver: Alan Swallow, 1959.

Theall, Donald F. "Traditional Satire in Eliot's 'Coriolan,'" *Accent*, XI (Autumn, 1951), 194-206.

Thérèse, Sister, S. N. D. "Hopkins' 'Spelt from Sibyl's Leaves,'" *Expl*, XVII (April, 1959), Item 45.

Thompson, Eric. *T. S. Eliot: The Metaphysical Perspective*. Carbondale: Southern Illinois University Press, 1963.

Tindall, William York. "James Joyce and the Hermetic Tradition," *JHI*, XV (January, 1954), 23-39.

———. *James Joyce: His Way of Interpreting the Modern World*. New York: Charles Scribner's Sons, 1950.

———. *The Literary Symbol*. New York: Columbia University Press, 1955.

———. *A Reader's Guide to James Joyce*. New York: Noonday, 1960.

Underhill, Evelyn. *Mysticism*. 12th ed., rev., 1930. London: Methuen, 1957.

Unger, Leonard. *T. S. Eliot*. University of Minnesota Pamphlets on American Writers. No. 8. Minneapolis: University of Minnesota Press, 1961.

Unterecker, John. "The Architecture of *The Bridge*," *WSCL*, III (Spring-Summer, 1962), 5-20.

Van Ghent, Dorothy. *The English Novel*. New York: Rinehart, 1953.

Vassilieff, Elizabeth. "The Quiddity of *Four Quartets*," *Direction*, No. 1 (May, 1952), 34-45.

Vergmann, Finn. " 'Ash Wednesday': A Poem of Earthly and Heavenly Love," *OL*, XIV (1959), 54-61.

Vickery, John B. "T. S. Eliot's Poetry: The Quest and the Way, Parts I and II," *Ren*, X (Autumn, 1957), 3-10; (Winter, 1957), 59-67.

Virginia, Sister Marie, O. P. "Some Symbols of Death and Destiny in *Four Quartets*," *Ren*, X (Summer, 1958), 187-191.

von Hügel, Friedrich. *The Mystical Element of Religion*. 2 vols. London: J. M. Dent and Sons and James Clarke, 1961.

Waggoner, Hyatt Howe. *The Heel of Elohim*. Norman: University of Oklahoma Press, 1950.

Wagner, Robert D. "The Meaning of Eliot's Rose-Garden," *PMLA*, LXIX (March, 1954), 22-33.

Wain, John. "Gerard Manley Hopkins: An Idiom of Desperation" (Chatterton Lecture on an English Poet), Read 13 May 1959, *Proceedings of the British Academy*, XLV (1959), 173-197.

Waith, Eugene M. "The Calling of Stephen Dedalus," *CE*, XVIII (February, 1957), 256-261.

Ward, Anne. "Speculations on Eliot's Time-world: An Analysis of *The Family Reunion* in Relation to Hulme and Bergson," *AL*, XXI (March, 1949), 18-34.

Ward, Dennis. " 'The Windhover,' " in *Interpretations*, ed. John Wain. London: Routledge and Kegan Paul, 1955.

Watkins, E. I. *Poets and Mystics*. New York: Sheed and Ward, 1953.

Weatherhead, A. Kingsley. "*Four Quartets:* Setting Love in Order," *WSCL*, III (Spring-Summer, 1962), 32-49.

Weber, Brom. *Hart Crane: A Biographical and Critical Study.* New York: Bodley, 1948.

Weigand, Elsie. "Rilke and Eliot: The Articulation of the Mystic Experience," *GR*, XXX (October, 1955), 198-210.

Weisstein, Ulrich. "*The Cocktail Party:* An Attempt at Interpretation on Mythological Grounds," *WR*, XVI (Spring, 1952), 232-241.

Weitz, Morris. "T. S. Eliot: Time as a Mode of Salvation," *SR*, LX (January-March, 1952), 48-64.

West, Ray B., Jr. "Personal History and the *Four Quartets*," *NMQ*, XXIII (Autumn, 1953), 269-282.

Whalley, George. *Poetic Process.* London: Routledge and Kegan Paul, 1953.

White, Helen C. *English Devotional Literature (Prose) 1600-1640.* University of Wisconsin Studies in Language and Literature. No. 29. Madison: University of Wisconsin Press, 1931.

————. *The Metaphysical Poets.* New York: Macmillan, 1956.

————. *The Tudor Books of Private Devotion.* Madison: University of Wisconsin Press, 1951.

Whitehead, Alfred North. *Science and the Modern World.* New York: Macmillan, 1926.

Wilder, Amos N. *The Spiritual Aspects of the New Poetry.* New York: Harper, 1940.

Williamson, George. *A Reader's Guide to T. S. Eliot.* New York: Noonday, 1957.

Willingham, John R. " 'Three Songs' of Hart Crane's *The Bridge:* A Reconsideration," *AL*, XXVII (March, 1955), 62-68.

————. "The Whitman Tradition in Recent American Literature." Unpublished doctoral dissertation, University of Oklahoma, 1953.

Wilson, Edmund. *Axel's Castle*. New York: Charles Scribner's Sons, 1931.

Wilson, Frank. *Six Essays on the Development of T. S. Eliot*. London: Fortune, 1948.

Wimsatt, W. K., Jr. "Eliot's Comedy," *SR*, LVIII (Autumn, 1950), 666-678.

Winter, Jack. " 'Prufrockism' in *The Cocktail Party*," *MLQ*, XXII (June, 1961), 135-148.

Winters, Yvor. *The Function of Criticism*. Denver: Alan Swallow, 1957.

————. *In Defense of Reason*. Denver: University of Denver Press, 1947.

Woodward, A. G. "Technique and Feeling in James Joyce's *A Portrait of the Artist as a Young Man*," *ESA*, IV (March, 1961), 39-53.

Wool, Sandra. "Weston Revisited," *Accent*, X (Autumn, 1950), 207-212.

Wooton, Carl. "The Mass: 'Ash Wednesday's Objective Correlative," *ArQ*, XVII (Spring, 1961), 31-42.

————. "The Terrible Fire of Gerard Manley Hopkins," *TSLL*, IV (Autumn, 1962), 367-375.

Wright, George. *The Poet in the Poem*. Berkeley: University of California Press, 1960.

.

Index

ascetic way, *see* asceticism
ascetical theology, *see* asceticism
asceticism, 2-11, 14, 16, 21-25, 34, 38-39, 75, 81, 91
Augustine, Saint, 5, 10, 56-61, 66, 146 n. 40

Basil, Saint, 6
Baudelaire, 147 n. 18
Beatrice, 46-53, 77-80, 93
Bernard, Saint, 19
Bhagavad-Gita, 93
Blake, 4, 144 n. 8
Blessed Virgin Mary, 11, 22-23, 25, 32, 38, 70, 77-79, 90, 93, 106, 120, 136, 138
Boehme, 148 n. 13
Bonaventure, Saint, 7
Browning, 4
Buddhism, 93
Butler, 7, 19

Calvacanti, 10
Camus, 130
charity, 7, 8, 17, 22-23, 29, 31, 35-37, 42-43, 51-52, 62-66, 69-71, 83-84, 87-89, 91, 92-93, 95-99, 128, 135-137, 139
Christianity, 1-2, 5-7, 11, 68-89, 93, 105-106, 109-116, 123-124, 126-129, 130-139
Coleridge, 4
Corvo, 38

Crane, 1-11, 29, 68, 74, 77-78, 80, 98, 102-129, 130-132, 137, 139

Dante, 6, 10, 45-54, 61, 68, 69, 70, 76-80, 82, 92, 93, 96, 146 n. 40
de Guibert, 2-3, 7, 81, 84
degrees of the spiritual life:
degree of beginners, *see* stages of the spiritual life, purgation
degree of proficients, *see* stages of the spiritual life, illumination
degree of the perfect, *see* stages of the spiritual life, union

Eliot, 1-11, 14, 23, 38, 72-101, 102, 108, 120, 125-126, 132-135, 137, 138-139
Emerson, 5

faith, 35-37, 42, 51-52, 55, 59, 83-84, 87-89, 92, 96, 98, 106-107, 115, 120
Fathers of the Church, 2, 5, 6
Faulkner, 130
Francis of Assisi, Saint, 41
Frank, 103, 114, 117, 122-123, 125

Garrigou-Lagrange, 14, 62, 81-82, 104
Gide, 130

175